# Displaced

## Our Lives So Differently Told

© 2011 Andy Evans & Vesna Kovac. All rights reserved

No part of this book may be reproduced, stored in retrieval system or transmitted by any means without the permission of
the authors

ISBN 978-1-4477-7967-4

# DISPLACED

Andy Evans & Vesna Kovac

About the Authors

Andy Evans was born in England – in one of Yorkshire's gritty coal mining communities.

After leaving school at the age of sixteen, he followed generations of school leavers before him to work in the local coal mines.

Following the demise of the UK's mining industry in the mid 1990s he now works within the Criminal Justice System.

Vesna Kovac was born and raised in the Bosnian Town of Novi Travnik.

From leaving school she graduated as an engineer, after studying for five years at the military academy in Zagreb.

She now lives in the USA with husband, Tonci, and sons, Nino and Tony.

Both writers came together following a twenty-year search to uncover family history intertwined with the country formerly known as Yugoslavia.

# Displaced

The book is dedicated to the everlasting memories of Maksim Ćulumović (Ćulum) and Petra Pljuco, without whom none of the words would have been possible.

\* \* \* \*

# Contents

| | |
|---|---|
| Chapter 1 | Early Years from Memory |
| Chapter 2 | Steps Taken Forwards |
| Chapter 3 | Re-Tossing the Coin |
| Chapter 4 | The Beginning of the End |
| Chapter 5 | Is There Anybody Out There? |
| Chapter 6 | Bosnia Old Country of Scars |
| Chapter 7 | In the Corner of Some Foreign Field |
| Chapter 8 | Walking in the Footsteps |
| Chapter 9 | Down This Road We've Been So Many Times |
| Chapter 10 | The long Road to Brđani |
| Chapter 11 | Away into the Uncertain Darkness |
| Chapter 12 | In the Corner Sat the Devil |
| Chapter 13 | Yesterdays Ghosts |
| Chapter 14 | Catching the Coin |
| Chapter 15 | The Other Side of the Coin |
| Chapter 16 | Memories of Early Years |
| Chapter 17 | Bratstvo – Welcome to the Machine |
| Chapter 18 | Did You See the Frightened Ones? |
| Chapter 19 | Switching off Humanity |
| Chapter 20 | Bratstvo – The End of the Dream |
| Chapter 21 | Heading East |

| | |
|---|---|
| **Chapter 22** | Heading West |
| **Chapter 23** | Love Amidst the Fear |
| **Chapter 24** | Women and War |
| **Chapter 25** | Hope at Last |
| **Chapter 26** | A Time for Healing |

## Acknowledgements and Thanks

Special thanks to the following for all the kind help and time given throughout my endless search:

Segeij and the kind people of the Serbian Genealogical Society / Srpsko Rodoslovno Društvo.

Roko – For all your help and patience which finally paid off when you made the final connection, enabling me to proceed and succeed with my search.

Vanja – Whose kind parents travelled to Brdani from their hometown of Mirkonjic Grad on my behalf and made the puzzle complete.

Mile and Mira – Who kindly invited me to Bosnia, allowing me to see - for the very first time - the things I had searched for so long.

Slavko and his father who kindly invited me into their homes in Šipovo, Bosnia.

Finally, a huge thank you goes out to the talented Kate Hughes for her proof reading and editing which was surely needed….. Thanks Kate

# Introduction

**Today we are offered information like** never before. At the click of a mouse we can purchase the latest computer hardware and software, order our weekly groceries, to be delivered to the door.

Even more impressive we can now retrieve records of the Uncle Frank we never before knew existed.

Genealogy for most is ingrained within our fabric. The desire to know where we originated from as never become greater. No more can I ever claim to be the age old slayer of giants to my young audience, nor will I ever be again the fighter of demons.
Alas now genealogy has put paid to such claims. Census records, readily available, at little cost, detail the true origins of our birth.

Whether we are of true blue blood origins, or the misfortunate product of a bygone shame, the records are now for all to see.

Just imagine now, if no records of our existence survived. As we turn around to face the high noon of the sun, no shadow will ever be cast to remind us we are truly alive and always were.

DISPLACED tells of such a search of no recordable beginning. Originally penned In Search of the Displaced Persons the story strives to uncover the shrouded blanket, kept in secret for over sixty years, of my own grandfather's life before his appearance in England in 1947. Yugoslavia's bloody and violent times of her past are revisited within my own travels of my modern day quest of understanding.

* * * *

# Part One - My Story

## Chapter One – Early Years from Memory

**Following the complete ceasefire of hostilities** in war-ravaged Europe, many hundreds of thousands of refugees found themselves displaced from their native homelands. A return to their respective country by most would often lead to persecution, torture and possible execution. The reasons for this were many but the most probable cause was they had simply fought to protect their people and homelands from the occupying German forces; as these were pushed back, the newly emerging communist regimes were being heavily supported by the encroaching Soviet army, replacing centuries old, exiting regimes and reshaping Europe for over half a decade.

Their recollections are countless and come from every country, once caught under the impregnable grip of the former iron curtain; however, , the story of my search centres on the now-independent countries of what was formerly Yugoslavia. Fifty year-old accounts of horror and suffering from its people have since been replaced with fresh horrors from the unimaginable carnage and bloodlust which erupted in the 1990s. Sadly, a country having once flourished beneath its socialist ideals, had torn itself apart with a vengeance, awakening centuries-old hatred within its people. Unfortunately, the break-up weighed enormously on the pressure of my relentless quest for information.

My search focuses on one individual who gave me so much in my early years - memories that will stay entwined within my being for eternity. There is not one memory from my childhood which does not feature his presence and even today, twenty years after his death, his influence and advice still fills my everyday life.

Looking back, a lot of this intrigue originated from the constant secrecy which seemed to follow him wherever he went. He was a man of very few words, making a seemingly miraculous appearance on earth in 1946 - at the birth age of thirty-seven. He seemed to me, as a child, the very fabric of hidden knowledge and deep understanding - a man who would draw those around him into his enveloping mystery. The fact that this deep and impenetrable aura could never be breached always added to the inner-rooted loyalty and connection has stayed with me to this very day.

Remarkably there were no recorded beginnings to the man I loved and respected. No uncles or cousins could be sought out to relay stories and anecdotes of the man as he had been in the youthful days of his prime. The shroud of secrecy enveloped me more and more as I slowly matured, the thirst for knowledge and understanding rising within me as each year passed. A desperate longing to simply know the very basics of the man engulfed me which would drive my quest for knowledge for the next twenty years.

I was not seeking out some worldwide conspiracy, nor was I searching for some unknown royal connection to turn the blood blue. I was simply seeking out simple answers to a man's existence prior to his displacement following the aftermath of World War Two.

My search has been extensive to say the least. From a humble start, following Granddad's death in 1988 to the use of Private Investigators, Handwriting Specialists and hours of searching internet files through to posting countless appeals on genealogical websites.

Over the years I'd come to the conclusion my search would never be answered. So many times I held my head in despair with the realisation my efforts would be inconclusive, was I simply searching for a man who had existed only in this country, from 1946. Steps taken forwards, sleepwalking back again - this always seemed to be the order of the day.

I would make progress only to face the stark realisation days later that the path I had chosen was leading me to unknown ground, and uncovered 'facts' did not necessary tally with what I already knew from memory, research, and commonsense.

The following pages not only detail my exhausting search but give an insight into what was my driving force: to uncover the veiled truth of one man's existence. From my humble beginnings - raised in a grim Yorkshire mining village where coal was king and the very essence of life centred on the colliery - to my visits to Bosnia and finally lifting the veil which had evaded my relentless twenty-year search.

There are stories from both sides of the coin; my recollections of a childhood spent with a man so obviously alien to his surroundings, to recollections of lost people spending the same years in their native land of Bosnia. Both sides of the coin never knew of the other's existence until the search was finalised; the passing of time at last embraced the reunion some sixty years after the coin was tossed for the very first time.

Featherstone is a town within the Wakefield District, in West Yorkshire, England, and stands south-west of Pontefract, boasting a population of 16,375.

Like many towns in the area, its birth grew in the Victorian industrial revolution. Coal was in constant demand to feed the greedy furnaces and boilers which were to make Britain Great. Lord Masham invested his wealth; three shafts were sunk into the virgin coal seams beneath the town's agricultural surface.

Migrant workers from the depleted Staffordshire coalfields fled to the newly-opened Yorkshire mines and Featherstone grew in prosperity and size. By the turn of the century, isolated farm houses had been replaced with the uniformity of back-to-back, terraced housing.

Unfortunately, Featherstone's rise was also tinged with sadness. During the uproar in 1893 the town came to national attention when soldiers fired on striking miners - killing two and injuring many others.

A distinctive sculpture, marking the centenary of the Featherstone Massacre, stands in the shopping precinct, and a large mural depicting the town's heritage can be seen at the town's main crossroads.

Sadly, Ackton Hall Colliery was the first pit to close following the end of the miners' strike of 1984 – 1985; unfortunately, this could not be contested as geological difficulties had made it impossible for the pit to continue production.

Despite most of the town's population growth taking place around the Industrial Revolution, Featherstone traces its history back much further than this. It is thought that a local public house, the Travellers' Rest, can trace its origins to the 17th century whilst the Jubilee Hotel, now sadly facing its death throes having been gutted by fire, is a listed building which once provided a resting place for wealthy Victorians and their horses.

'It always rains on a Sunday', I would say to myself as I looked out of the window. 7 a.m. and already woken by the sounds of Granddad busying himself making breakfast - usually cheese and fresh eggs (laid within the hour) and cooked to perfection in the coal-fired Yorkshire stove.

I would watch with intrigue as I ate. Stripped to the waist standing at the kitchen sink. The bear-like man before me would scrub away traces of his earlier labour, working the soil in his beloved allotment. It was the same ritual each and every morning - neck, chest, and armpits, before he too sat and ate the result of his endeavours.

He would take time to sit with me at the veneered table by the window in the large kitchen which also acted as a day to day living room. Despite having spent thirty years living in England he had never truly mastered the language. The east European accent remaining strong within his words made him difficult to understand to those not accustomed to his voice.

Sparrows always fascinated me, each time I looked out of the window of the bedroom I had at my grandparents' house overlooking Gladstone Street. The tiny, drab coloured birds would busy themselves in their daily lives, seemingly oblivious to the rigours of everyday life in the little town they inhabited.

The feathered mice, as they were referred to, would hurriedly feed their young chicks with scraps offered from many of the houses' breakfast tables – left-overs of bacon rind and bread.

Sparrows of my generation seemed to live a very unhealthy lifestyle of fatty foods. How they flew, I do not know to this day. 1970s Featherstone was a world away from the healthy eating bigots of nowadays. Perhaps nowadays a stringent programme of exercise and low fat diet would be imposed on our feathered friends. Strangely, however, since the arrival of commercially-packaged bird food, there seems a distinct lack of 'chirping' amidst the gutters and rooftops of Featherstone.

Its strange how one memory in particular stays embedded in our thoughts for no particular reason, and which will manifest itself, whenever the strange tricks of the human mind automatically regresses, with flickering images of one's existence. A catastrophic event I am able to recall would be welcome in adult conversations on childhood memories, but no, sparrows, rainfall and bacon rind will always, I fear, be the essence of my early years.


There are many books around today written about local history, especially the sprawling expanse of the northern mining communities which were the heart and soul of Britain's prosperity. My own story, in its beginning, will merely scratch on the surface of this proud heritage, now in its final demise. However, the pages will focus on a primary socialisation which changed the course of events entirely for me, as I developed and nurtured the fires which provided my motivation to pen these chapters and finally seek the truth.

Featherstone, today, is far from the meagre stance of only forty five years ago when my own eyes opened for the very first time. To have skin other than the whitest of white, meant the holder had not bathed in the pit-head baths following his working day at the colliery. Any foreign accent would be associated with the speaker hailing from a neighbouring county, here to reap the rewards of the promising wages paid from the prospering Yorkshire coalfield.

My recollections of childhood were those of happy times. Featherstone seemed like a warm pillow of protection which I embraced, finding comfort from its genial, happy people. Everyone seemed to know each other, help each other and care for each other. I even recall funerals fondly as a child; the whole street would have a certain 'buzz' on the particular morning.

Women would scrub the steps leading up to the front doors of their houses. The immediate street surface would be cleansed with hot soapy water, chasing away any traces of grime before the cortège appeared, in respect for the sad passing of a dear neighbour. It almost seemed like a competition - who would have the cleanest steps - to be remembered for eternity by the departed.

Childhood memories are filled with endless days of self-taught amusement. Games often transpired from mere imagination, adapted through the passing of time ensuring they kept to the latest trends and were fashionable.

Hide and seek, kick out can and the constant re-enactment of fiercely fought Hollywood battles between warring factions from World War Two were always popular. To children like us these were the games offering hours and days of rich amusement.

Looking back now, it is sad to see the once-favourite haunts of endless generations of happy-go-lucky children now deserted and derelict.

Shortcuts and woodland have now receded back to the clutches of nature as hurriedly-running feet now tend to stay within the confines of relative safety, by street-lit paths and roads. Computers and gaming stations have replaced the plastic rifles and empty aluminium cans. The gathering of adolescents on street corners is now frowned upon and seen more of an annoyance. By today's modern standards I guess we were poor people, but most importantly, we were happy people. In retrospect, I feel it was so nice to be poor.

The colliery spoil heap has long since gone. Landscaping has now transformed the surrounding area into woodland and grazing for cattle. Long gone are the days of fun and mirth - the intrepid mountain climber, beating the forbidden heights; the astronaut surveying the lunar landscape for the very first time; the final, secret mission to elude the enemy, all now gone. Once again, Mother Nature has been given back what was rightfully hers.

Like many northern coal-mining towns, Featherstone was lacking in amenities to say the least. Public Houses and Working Men's Clubs were the prominent feature of leisure time and were usually busy centres for the local community.

These 'dens of ill repute' had prospered, quenching the eternal thirsts of the hard working, hard playing miners.

The younger generations were catered for by the many sporting activities enjoyed - in the form of Rugby League, soccer and cricket.

Rugby League, however, took precedence. Like most northern mining towns, Featherstone was, and remains, steeped in rugby tradition.

Post Office Road remains the spiritual home of the town. Childhood heroes, Vince Farrar, Arnie Morgan and Phil Butler, to name a few, once trod the sacred turf of my yesterdays.

The more senior residents tended to take solace in the many stretches of available plots of land, or allotments, as these were known. They made good use of the plots, and enjoyed the fresh air - a respite from the harsh reality of coal mining.

These were 'Royal Lands' or 'Dutchy' as they were commonly called; a gift from the Royal family to the working man. Just a few pounds annually transformed the common man into a land owner. The allocated strip of workable soil was his own to do with as he pleased.

These plots of land were usually the pride and joy of the allotment keeper; vegetables and fruits were grown and poultry were reared. The often obsessive sport of pigeon racing was also indulged.

Granddad's particular allotment or plot of land would become another deeply embedded chapter in the annals of my particular memories, from both my primary and secondary socialisation.

Perhaps it didn't actually *always* rain on Sundays; I spent so much time there amongst the vegetable and fruits and recall it always being bathed in sunshine. The air would be filled with the song of the skylark from neighbouring farmland. Shrieks of dismay always followed from the disturbed blackbird roused from its security, hidden deep within the neatly cut hedgerow.

Granddad's space was so different from those of the neighbouring plots. Usually these allotments were a mishmash of collective junk. Old doors acted as fences or lack lustre attempts at keeping nature's wild growth at bay.

Whenever you entered this space you were transported away from the grit and grime of Featherstone. This was Alice Through The looking Glass, without the novel. Everything was transformed into a place so alien to its surroundings. The collection of huts and sheds were constructed in such a way that I would not see again until my journey to Bosnia.

Everything in this magical plot was done to such a high standard, almost perfection. You entered through a panelled door cutting its way through a boundary hedge - which was always trimmed in exact straight lines.

So exact had the line to be that I recall him once returning home in deep sadness. Engrossed in surveying and cutting back the prosperous growth of budding leaves he had failed to see the rising heads of the nestling blackbirds. To the innocent, naïve fledglings' disturbance of the leafy canopy above their heads meant food. Today however had been quite different. Stretching up their necks in readiness for the offered worm from the parent bird had brought only death.

Innocently the five blackbirds of tomorrow were decapitated with one innocent snap of the steel pruning shears.

Distraught, Granddad would always, in future, carefully inspect the line of hedgerow for wildlife before the operation of neatness could begin.

Hedges were a target for us children and we would leap into them in a childish frenzy, to be ejected at speed with the force of their natural ability to spring back into place. Not this hedge - it, for some reason, was never targeted. It was "Max's hedge" and avoided at all cost.

Once through the door it would fascinate me each and every time just how perfect and meticulously tidy the plot of land was. Everything was carefully planned, from the grassed path running in a straight line central to the plots of vegetables, to the boundary fences. All manner of vegetables and fruits were grown here, from the native plants of England, to tobacco. Never before, nor have I since, seen tobacco plants grown in this country. The leaves were harvested in late summer and hung to dry in my grandfather's wooden huts, giving off a pungent odour that, at times, I can occasionally smell today when I enter a room. Harvest time, I recall, was a time of excitement for me. Armed with a curved blade, I would be given free realm to chop down the giant plants. Briefly I was the lumberjack, working the forest slopes.

The crowning glory to me as a child, however, would have to be the huge greenhouse I fondly called the Crystal Palace due to its imposing construction.

This must have been twenty metres in length by eight metres in width and was heated by water pipes fed from a coal-burning stove. Stifling heat would greet you each and every time you entered this sacred space. Combined with this heat the pungent aroma of tomatoes made it difficult to take in deep breaths and, as a child I would retreat back through the sealed door ever fearing I would be overcome and collapse.

Tomatoes grown here were renowned for their flavour. Summer school holidays for me were spent selling these door to door from a huge, wooden wheelbarrow. I recall the demand for these always outweighed how quickly they ripened - the wheelbarrow emptied faster than it could be restocked with carefully weighed produce.

Granddad is still fondly remembered by Featherstone's more senior residents for the tomatoes he produced.


Many memories stay ingrained from childhood and these are simply ripples on the surface that immediately rise to the forefront of my mind, whenever I think back to his life. What I do recall is an individual who seemed to stand out from any crowd he was part of; a man who seemed to summon respect amongst his own nationals, reinforcing the secrecy surrounding him.

Children would offer him this same respect and be on their best behaviour whenever he was in their presence. Strangely, as my research drew to a close, it was interesting to find that the brother who had survived in Bosnia had these same traits and characteristics, despite the two being cut apart some forty years before their deaths.

Simple forms of identical body language, how they stood

and held their arms, to the preference of how they wore their hats, all appeared to survive the passing of time and remained part of the very essence uniting true brotherhood. A connection which remained so deeply embedded into their very fabric - which the isolation from each other had not been able to destroy.

*   *   *   *

# Displaced

## Our Lives So Differently Told

# Chapter Two – Steps Taken Forwards - Sleepwalking Back Again

**Featherstone in the late 1940's would have** been a very foreboding and miserable place, even for its native inhabitants socialised from birth, to a life of Victorian squalor and the rigours of coal mining.

Displaced refugees were eagerly accepted by the post-war government, to replace the indigenous labour force which had perished in the war. Any individual was seen as simply that, a worker to replace one no longer there.

Exploitation was here on a grand scale. The displaced refugees from war-torn Europe simply had no choice - either accept the stringent conditions set out by the host government or simply return to their native countries and face possible death. Life can deal, at times, a cruel hand - the hand of all games played with human life in which my own country participated. Life for a life here literally meant just that.

Three-year contracts were signed to the Ministry of Labour. Either the participant honoured their three-year contract of designated work, or they would be returned, immediately, to their respective homelands.

Lies would often be told in the hope the newcomer would be more appealing to any prospective employer. It was commonplace for individuals to shed years from their actual age to make themselves more likely to be offered employment. I heard, first-hand, of such stories when I began my own mining career. Elderly Polish miners would admit freely to lying about having mining experience in their native homeland.

Coal mining was king in Yorkshire and miners were needed to hew the coals. This was regardless of experience in the industry so all were sent to graze the offered pasture.

The newcomers to our country were met with obvious glee from the newly nationalised coal industry. The government now had a seemingly endless supply of green labour to fulfil the demands, fuelling Britain's economy once more following the ceasefire of hostilities.

Upon arrival in the UK from displaced persons' camps in Italy and Germany, the new arrivals were then dispersed into the many camps that had been hurriedly readied for them across the country. Miners' Hostels had been created during the war years to house the 'Bevin Boys'. Bevin Boys were young British men who were conscripted to work in the coal mines to replace the workforce drafted into the armed forces. From 1943 until 1948 nearly 48,000 Bevin Boys performed vital, but largely unrecognised, service in the mines.

With the men now returning after fighting a good cause, these hostels lay dormant and so in an act of natural progression were put to good use. The Miners' Hostel was replaced with the Displaced Persons camp, once again filling the dormitories with laughter and conversation. This time, however, the walls resounded with words of which they were not accustomed. Ukrainian, Polish and the tongue of the Yugoslavian now echoed along the corridors.

Maksim Ćulumović was initially held at Full Sutton Camp, near the city of York, in North Yorkshire after his arrival in the United Kingdom in 1947. The camp, like many others, was crudely planned and the Displaced Persons were made up of many different nationalities from across Europe.

Little, if indeed any thought had been given to the huge differences between individuals there. Devout enemies were placed together. Maybe the post-war government was hoping that with the world at peace, old feuds would be forgotten. It is interesting to read, during one sitting in the House of Commons, a debate took place regarding the behaviour towards each other of the displaced persons at Full Sutton Camp.

Strangely too, the only photograph I possess of Granddad from his days at this camp shows obvious bruising to his left eye.

At Full Sutton, the Ministry of Labour processed the internees and, like many others he was designated to work in the coal mining industry. Before any employment could begin, the men and women had to be taught basic English. Each day they would be driven to a nearby learning centre in the village of Pocklington. Once they were able to understand the rudimentary elements of their new language, individuals were then dispatched to hostels near to their allocated places of work.

Granddad was initially sent to a Miners' Hostel, at Askern, in South Yorkshire, where he underwent the basic training required to work underground at the local colliery.

Once this 'short-cut' training was complete, he was again moved to the Miners' Hostel at High Town in Castleford, within two miles of the designated colliery at Fryston, located on the outer fringes of the town. He continued to work underground until his retirement at the age of sixty-five, despite having his back broken during an underground collapse.

It appears he was a well-liked individual amongst his fellow miners. Standing out from the others due to him wearing a thick fur coat underground. He would rally the new mining recruits plucked early from their years of schooling and remind them just how lucky they were to have been born and raised in England.

To Granddad, being taken from the breast of family life at the age of thirteen to enter the depths of old king coal was nothing. To be taken away to fight a war was another, never to be judged along the same lines of suffering.

As the slow passing of childhood years changed gear and seemed to accelerate away from me, I found myself becoming more intrigued with the man whom had played a central role in my early upbringing.

Teenage years beckoned, and I would spend more and more time around this man I looked up to and respected so much. Granddad "Max", it was obvious to me, found great solace in the fact that here was a kid who not only held so much adoration for him, but also yearned to be included in the fabric of his life.

At times, it felt to me as if I was being moulded to represent cherished ones from a family long since gone, never to return from a land far away and unknown to me. I knew the part I was to play, and was happy this role had been offered from a figure in my life I adored and respected so much. Deep down within me, I knew this was how it was meant to be.

Maybe the fuel for the fire of the deeply rooted connection between us was the unknown element which seemed to envelop him in a veiled mist.

To be displaced entirely from your natural surroundings must be the cruellest blow ever to be experienced. Life is built on experience and memory, to have these taken away must be like having the very soul of your existence torn out, to be replaced with a blank page of knowing nothing, only what could have been and would never be again.

Here was a man who had arrived in the United Kingdom in 1946, at the birth age of thirty-six years. Nothing gave away his story prior to this overdue birth. No fond recollections or anecdotal stories of youth and happiness would ever be spoken to amuse an audience over food and drink.

Here was a mystery man who had simply no past that could be joined with his present and future to create a natural path of existence and presence. When the man left this second beginning it was obvious the first would be erased forever; with his death the story would never be told.

There would be no turning back, as I found over the last twenty years of searching out the answers that were never given to my questions, despite relentless asking. Time always moves forward, we cannot stop or reverse it, no matter how strong the wish.

Maksim was a book forever closed, a book which would meet its sad demise long before it would be found, opened and read.

How I have wished for all these years that the answers to my humble questions had been resolved in his life-time, rather than having to endlessly trawl through the 'maybes' and 'ifs' following his death.

So much easier, but I guess ease is often out of our reach, and to find the whole truth we sometimes have to look even closer, eliminating the fiction from the fact.

'Who really are you?' I would ask constantly over a breakfast of fresh eggs and toasted bread. The answer would always be the same: simply, 'I am Max.' Max, a closed book with only the conclusion left to be written.

His life was a guarded secret at all times. The key had been turned and discarded forever; perhaps only ever to be turned again in the final moments of my own exhausting search, years later.

Occasionally he would let his shield slip momentarily and offer a slight glimpse into the man he had been, allowing only the shortest of gazes into his memory. These short, unguarded lapses were usually over the table at meal times, and would be retracted as quickly as they had been offered.

On one occasion, I recall he spoke about his early childhood. With a wide grin beaming across his face, he went on to say he had been breastfed until he was seven years old. He expanded, with the slightest of smiles explaining mother would hide away from him as he searched for her to be fed.

The hungry child, eager for breast milk from his mother, weary in the passing of her years, and who could yield no more.

On another occasion, he spoke of a childhood memory of a brother, older than himself - how they would make cigarettes from dried corn husks and hide out of view, so they could smoke them in the trees surrounding their little village.

They would steal Slivovitz from the family home, hiding in the nearby woods, getting hopelessly drunk, (Slivovitz is a distilled beverage made from damson plums. It is frequently called plum brandy and is part of the category of drinks called Rakia).

The darkest of memories he briefly offered was of the night his world had been changed forever.

He spoke of a night attacking militia had led the occupying forces to the houses where he and his family lived. He recalled whilst the occupying troops surrounded the dwellings, the militia men had shot and beaten to death everyone they came across, without mercy. With great sadness, he recalled seeing his own son being tethered and then cut to death by the laughing invaders. This is the very last memory he offered for the rest of his life – so distant to the other half of him that had been born, raised and loved in those foreign parts.

I was later to learn with horror and sadness that Granddad had merely exposed the briefest of glimpses into the true barbarity mankind is capable of unleashing onto its own.

As my own searching concluded I would hear first-hand accounts from elderly local people of the true horrors of war.

The conquering German and Italian armies re-awoke centuries-old hatreds within Yugoslavia's mixed and varied people. The fuse paper was lit, and overnight, age-old religious and cultural divides were once again exposed. Neighbours were transformed into haters, and overnight the hilly slopes were bathed in blood.

Ageing survivors recalled, from the mists of time, that no mercy had been shown to any man, woman, or child. Women had gathered their children together in sheer panic and attempted to evade the attackers by reaching mountain slopes south of the village. Only barbarity and inhumanity met them along their frenzied attempt to escape.

Stories still prevail how Mothers had drowned their own children in the depths of the nearby river before taking their own lives. Unfortunates who were unlucky to fall into the militia men's hands were cruelly tortured and mutilated. Bodies of children were strewn across the woodland slopes, some having the amputated breasts of their Mothers placed in their mouths in a final act of human savagery.

It saddens me to write of such inhuman horror. At this point in my research I had looked only at the beauty of Yugoslavia. Now the country had become ugly; a place of murder and betrayal. Twenty years later, within my own search, I would finally uncover the truth.

In essence, the beauty had become soiled with horror. Not only had neighbour turned against neighbour, but husband had turned against wife. Ethnic and religious boundaries had been set overnight. The bloodshed was to last another four long years.

What I always found strange in these short and rare glimpses into Granddad's memories was that he would never speak of names. Even when prompted for names of the people he fondly spoke about, he would instantly switch and speak of other things, never to be persuaded back to the earlier conversation.

My parents fondly recall they would intentionally ply him with his beloved whiskey in attempts at dropping his guard. Whatever the reason however, his secrecy always proved too strong, and he always knew their plan. He would disappear to bed when he realised his guard was slipping in the mists of a drunken stupor.

Whatever horrors lurking beneath the surface of Grandfather's memory would occasionally find their way to the surface in his sleep. Mam recalls that, as a child, she would be woken in the small hours by the sounds of his screams, as he relived his past experiences whilst in deep slumber.

Mam also recalls she would forever ask two of Grandfather's closest friends, both displaced from what was formerly Yugoslavia, about anything which would give a clue to the mystery. Again, this proved to be fruitless. It was as if there was a code of silence that had to be adhered to. The answer, she recalled, would always be the same: "Ask Max - if he wants you to know then he will tell you."

Looking back I still find it impossible to comprehend. How could a man who had suffered so much in his own life, show so much love and tenderness to others? Whatever hatreds and need for revenge he carried with him had been deeply confined, never once to rear their heads in anger. Maybe the human mind simply locks away and archives memories to give hope to a continued and normal existence.

Looking back, my recollections are always of a fiercely independent man who never asked for anything. He never seemed able to fully adjust to his surroundings and the English way of life.

He would do things either his way or not at all. At times, I feared he would continue with things which he had started, regardless of whether he thought they were truly right or not. If he thought at the beginning that he was right then right he would have to be until the end - whether the final outcome was positive or negative. He would never admit however, yes, perhaps, he had been wrong after all.

Every project he undertook, whether work within the house, or constructing something on the allotment, was painstakingly carried out by hand. I can never recall seeing him use a power tool of any description, despite these being readily available at a reasonable cost.

Although nothing was ever completed to a craftsman's finish, he certainly built things to last the rigours of time. I remember adopting a young hawk whose parents had abandoned it. With nowhere to keep the fledgling predator of the skies Granddad immediately went to work. Suddenly wood appeared as if by magic from nowhere and within days a structure had been erected. Maybe Granddad had simply misheard or understood just how large the bird would grow. Whether hawks in his native homeland were indeed capable of carrying bulls to the slaughter, or whether ingrained instinct had taken over with the construction. Taking centre stage now in the small garden was a structure well capable of wintering out a small flock of sheep. Cosmetically poor in appearance, its strength and longevity far outweighed its negatives.

Probably the most memorable feat of construction I remember was the well he dug to access the water table on the allotment. This always amazed me - both as a child and also the last time I saw it some five years ago.

The well was maybe thirty feet in depth and perhaps just over two feet in diameter. Its construction was square, and impeccably, the whole of its depth was lined by brickwork. Water was drawn from the depths with a bucket lowered and raised from a wooden pendulum. On the other end there had been a small barrel weighted with bricks, to ease raising the water-filled bucket.

I remember the water always being ice cold, regardless of the heat from the summer sun. In today's fashionable market for bottled water, maybe an empire could have been built from this free and inexhaustible commodity.

If at any time I hear mention of a well I am always taken back to the summer of 1977. The summer in question was a particularly hot one, down on records as such.

Britain was in the grip of drought and water was rationed. Communal taps had been installed, rather than the diminishing water supply being fed to individual houses across many of our towns and cities.

Like most young kids in my area, I was the proud owner of an ancient air rifle. I would spend hours on the allotment, shooting at anything from rusty tin cans, to targets drawn on the boundary fences, and would idle away the long summer holidays from school losing myself in the thought that I was one of the all time master sharpshooters.

One day, during the long August holiday of that unbearably hot year (which was too hot for the usual games of cricket and soccer which would normally occupy the long Summer days for us bored teenagers), I decided on the order of the day - after watching the repeated offerings which made up children's television - would have to be the allotment with its solace. Also, perhaps more importantly, the gentle, cooling breeze and long shadows it offered, would give at least some respite from the perpetually blazing sun.

Armed with rifle in hand, lead pellets as ammunition, and four pints of water from the emergency communal tap, I set off for a day's forage and adventure.

The simple collier boy had become the freedom fighter once more. Like his Grandfather, he was both feared and revered. Unlike him however, this was just a game - a game where only one could ever be victorious. A game where true pain and longing were never felt.

The journey passed uneventfully. This was not unusual as the allotment was situated a mere twenty metres form my parents' house.

As usual, upon reaching my destination, I found the old panelled door to my chosen hunting ground was unlocked. Granddad would, I guessed, have been here already, as soon as the sun gave enough light for him to see. Even the door or gateway was mysterious. The allotments were a poor man's escape from reality. Fervently improvised attempts to seal the gardener's kingdom were sometimes feeble to say the least.

Fences, bordering on being both fragile and incompetent, ruled my landscape. Old, weather-beaten doors, once opened to allow in the festive cheer of families long since gone, were now mere portals to the vegetable patch.

As I made my way into the haven of lush flora, it always amazed me just how much life there was amidst the scorched surroundings, the vegetation that had succumbed to dehydration.

Despite my calling, and walking the entire breadth of the enclosed allotment, Granddad was nowhere to be seen. A stroke of luck, perhaps on my part. The usual rusting tin can may not be the only chosen target in his absence, I thought, as I eyed a passing starling who perched, preening iridescent plumage as it landed on a nearby fence.

The wilful killing of any bird in the allotment was totally outrageous in Granddad's eyes and was always met with rage. He saw them as a gardener's friend, an ally to help combat the myriads of tiny creatures that invaded his space and who dared to take microscopic bites of his cherished cabbages.

"What eyes do not see, eyes will not know," I whispered, as I gently raised the air rifle in the direction of the unwary target - still busily tending its feathers and enjoying the morning sunshine.

Slowly now, ever so slowly, the rifle's sights steadied on the poor, unsuspecting, feathered gardener's friend. The deadly assassin, now in the zone, had been trained. With forefinger trembling I began to squeeze down on the trigger......

"Help! Help me!" Came the eerie voice from beneath my feet.

I recall being so shaken by this unexpected sound that I dropped the rifle to the ground, forcing the trigger mechanism to operate and send the lead projectile skywards without aim or chance of connection with the target.

I looked around; everything was as it should be. I was alone but quite sure I had heard a distinctive voice calling for help. Maybe memories distort over the passing of time but if you were to ask me now I would swear it was the poor starling - in what could have been its final moment, asking to be spared.

Steadying myself, and regaining the composure of a brave sharpshooter, I picked up the discarded rifle, reloading it with another lead pellet before scanning the surroundings for my next precision shot.

All was quiet; no feathered foes were in my eager sight so I proceeded further into the allotment. Stealth was now the key in my quest for action, so progress was cautious and slow.

"Help me someone!" came the mysterious voice again, but this time it appeared to come from the ground all around me.

Although the words were recognisable, I recall thinking it sounded like that of Hollywood spirits from some black and white movie, screened late on Friday evenings. The echoed sound was a mixture between voice and breeze, as if its very essence was in the warm, subtle wind which drifted slowly all around.

This time there was no mistaking it, this was a voice that sounded so very distant but so very near. Not from one direction, as if someone was calling, but from everywhere.

"Ghost!" I remember thinking, as I turned and ran as fast as my legs could carry me. Not just a ghost but the devil himself, I thought, as I stood, gasping for breath once outside the now forbidding confines of the imposing allotment. This was now my very own appointment with fear.

Slowly the sharpshooter's pride returned once more. Fearing the essence of the day's adventure had been lost, or rather scared out of me, I returned the thirty or forty steps home, hung my rifle to rest and, like all intrepid adventurers, asked Mam what time dinner would be ready.

Thankfully, the rest of the day was uneventful. No visitations from long dead spirits crept from the shadows and it was possible that the afternoon's television was not too fraught with repeated films and Walt Disney cartoons. Lassie, the wonder dog, no doubt would have saved another poor soul from danger and Skippy, the Bush Kangaroo, would have been able to make his human owner aware of possible danger. Afternoon sandwiches, washed down with fizzy dandelion and burdock, would finalise the day.

I recall it being around 7p.m. when Nana made the journey from her side of the street to ours. She had met Granddad whilst working at the Miners' Hostel in Castleford and immediately the couple had forged an unbreakable bond.

Co-habiting in those days had been regarded as a sin but Nana accepted, through sheer love of the man, that Granddad would never marry her. Marriage, he maintained, would make him a British National. He was a Yugoslav and would take his true ethnicity to the grave.

Stubbornness was his virtue. I was to learn in the years leading to his death, my parents had begged him to obtain a British passport so they could take him to his homeland once more. He refused, and said if he were to return to Yugoslavia he would return as a Yugoslav and not as a British tourist.

Nana was frantic when she came, asking if anyone had seen 'Max'.

Apparently, he had left as usual at daybreak for the allotment and had not returned, not even for his beloved Teachers whiskey, which was his very lifeblood back then. No one had seen him at all throughout the day, and, after another trip to the allotment, it was decided he was well and truly missing.

After telephoning the police, I recall we sat and discussed the possible scenarios. Only one thing was possible, he'd had a jackpot win on his beloved horse racing, and was blind drunk somewhere.

Back then, a telephone call to the local constabulary usually meant that an officer would attend within a reasonable time and, true to form, there soon came the obligatory 'policeman's knock' at the door.

"Hello, hello, hello," would be, from memory, the police's response to any enquiry, but I cannot remember the exact words. Maybe my memory has become clouded with the passing of time, but I like to think had been the stereotypical policeman's announcement of his presence in the 1970's.

After a brief discussion, the search began on the still-unlocked allotment. Within minutes, the ghostly voice resounded throughout the air. Again, communicating the same appeal of, "Help me!". Maybe the police officer was not an ardent believer in the spirit world, for he continued with his search uninterrupted, like a detective sleuth on the trail of a jewel thief.

No sooner had the search started than it was over. Standing over the exposed well, the officer called us over and, with the aid of his flashlight, revealed a rather dishevelled Granddad, maybe ten feet below, wedged tight against the brickwork.

After much heaving with the aid of an old, oily length of rope, Granddad was hoisted to safety. Battered and bruised from his ordeal, he explained the well had been dry; he suspected this may have been caused by a blockage, and had climbed down to investigate. He had lost his footing and fell, only to come to a stop when he had become wedged tightly against the brickwork.

I recalled, with a smile, the ghostly voices from earlier, and the penny dropped. That is why the noise seemed to come from everywhere. It was being transmitted through the empty, underground waterway, and surfaced everywhere the ground offered escape.

As teenage years beckoned, the magnetic bond that held me and my grandfather so close seemed to strengthen. I found myself wanting so desperately to discover the true man who had played such a significant part in my early years.

The tide of time was slowly turning and I now found myself wanting to draw back the veil around the man, rather than just be beckoned to the fascination which always surrounded him because he was so different.

With the passing of childhood years came the acquired knowledge I had gleaned from spending time browsing the pitiful array of books in the local libraries. Anything having the merest of information regarding Yugoslavia would be taken home and read.

The information was scant, to say the least, and probably quite antiquated in its content. The 1970's were the dawn of the package holiday, when the ardent traveler would relish the dream of exotic places like France and Spain. Yugoslavia, to the majority, was still far beyond the realms of perception for all but the intrepid, and the devout explorers of a western world who were ignorant to anything encroaching upon the once-iron curtain of the east.

Foreign language lessons at school were now becoming commonplace, focusing mostly on French, Spanish and German.

After all, if we were meant to travel to such extreme places as the out-of-reach Balkans, these languages would surely have been placed within our reach during the most precious years of our education.

Despite the odds being stacked against me, I was slowly arming myself with the desperate information I desired. Yugoslavia, I read, was a beautiful place of mountains, forests, fauna and, above all else, mystery.

Despite the very basic information those feeble books offered, and through the aura that followed Granddad around, I always seemed to connect with a place I had never seen.

They say some people have the gift to somehow feel the background image of someone through only their presence. Maybe this is true in all of us, for I could always sense distant images of places so alien to me whenever I was in his company. Some call it our sixth sense, a natural part of our inner ability which has become lost to most.

Opening the heavy door to the allotment, I would always feel removed instantly from the surroundings I knew so well. The skylark would continue her summer song overhead and the whispery, bellowing steam clouds would continue to rise into the blue sky from the nearby power station.

Here before me, however, was something different- the soil, laden with nature's treasure trove of vegetables and fruits. Only a moment ago I had been surrounded by King Coal at its worst. Smoke, dust and noise pollution reigned supreme.

Granddad would praise adoration for his true god, Mother Nature. She must have received love ten-fold and it was obvious, from the surrounding greenery, his true loyalty was paid back in full.

Like most kids of the time, I was interested in war games and battles of old. Unlike most kids, however, I was always the odd-soldier-out in the streets of Featherstone.

Whenever the greatest battles were replayed, and before the first make-believe shot had been fired, sides were drawn. These were fairly simple to decide, always a victorious British commando or the defeated German storm trooper. Not so easy, however, whenever I was drawn into the conflict of warfare.

"What side?" I recall they always asked, "Us, or them?" My reply would always be the same – "Yugoslavia". As usual, I would be left to my own devices and, given no support in the ensuing battle, would simply fight my own guerrilla war against everyone.

Looking back, it still surprises me how many actual battles young Yugoslavia was victorious in, given the fact that I was one against many.

Although I do not recall any specific influence I may have been directly exposed to, it is obvious Granddad had ingrained his beliefs and feelings into me as a child. By the time I was in the latter stages of teenage years, I understood, and believed, most importantly, that Granddad had been served a great injustice. What he so loyally fought for had been swept away cruelly, and he'd carried this heavy burden through the rest of his lifetime.

He was always fragmented in his answer to any question. He had built an impenetrable wall of defence which became sealed and, whatever his reasons, was taken with him to the grave.

Slowly, I accumulated, from the fragments of information offered, he had fought during World War II and had suffered the harshest of conditions, living from day to day in the vast mountain ranges that made up Yugoslavia. His tears at the memories of his son, and the murderous troops that lay waste to his village were ever present in my memory.

I recall too that he despised, bitterly, Britain's war-time Prime Minister, Winston Churchill. He would fly into a rage whenever he was shown on television. Again, he never gave reason for this, only that Churchill had been responsible for the deaths of so many of his people.

With later reading I have found Winston Churchill, a staunch, one-time supporter of the Yugoslav people, had switched his allegiance overnight to that of Josip Broz's (Tito) communist partisans, and had sealed the fate for thousands of fighters in Yugoslavia.

A fate which would inevitably end, like their leader, in death.

It is sad that a man can live his life without having any past; a past he can share amongst the people he loved so deeply. Life is built on memories, and not being able to pass on memories of one's life must have been painful and without relief.

The only past he had for the world was locked away within him, and those of his own kind who had suffered the same fate. The slightest glimpse of this past could be found in an old suitcase he kept locked upstairs in the house. Looking into the suitcase was deeply forbidden and would be met with anger if ever he found it had been opened.

Despite the danger, I would often creep and peek inside with fingers shaking, in fear of being caught. Within these confines was the man I had never known. I remember letters, their hand in some strange language unknown to me, photographs of people never known, and passports. I will always remember that. Why should one man have so many passports?

The case was a closed book, like Maksim. Whenever the lid was sealed, so too was the man.

I recall, in sadness, opening the case for the very last time, after his death. It was so empty - like his memories. Most of the contents had been removed, as if he'd known his fast approaching fate and had brushed over his footprints, hiding his path forever.

Remaining within the confines of the old case were photographs of women and children - bearing writing in Serbian on the back of each picture. A collection of resettlement papers and a brass military emblem, which appeared to be a military cap badge and two gold and mother of pearl uniform buttons, were also left behind.

Only one of these photographs had ever been shown to me by Granddad. I remember having coffee there when he came into the living room and put the photograph on the table, tapping it with his finger to draw my attention.

"Which one am I?" he asked, as he glanced at me with a wry smile.

The photograph was that of a group of uniformed men, some sat, others standing, with one lying down at the forefront. The person lying down was in military uniform and the brass military badge in my possession could be clearly seen upon his cap.

I recall the smile as he pointed at this figure and simply said, "Maksim".

No sooner had the photograph appeared than it was picked up and taken back upstairs to the safety of its protective suitcase.

Intrigued by this strange act with the photograph, I attempted to coax him into conversation about his exploits during World War II. I remember asking him what rank he held. I started with corporal and he motioned his hand as if to say higher; sergeant, I asked, again the hand motioned higher but this time he laughed, turned and left the room. The conversation was over.

49

The next time I was to see the photograph would be five or six years later following his death. Strangely, it had been defaced. Individuals' faces had been erased, caused by intentional scratches on the paper, as if vital clues had been removed.

* * * *

# Displaced

## Our Lives So Differently Told

## Chapter Three – Re-Tossing the Coin
### Maksim Ćulumović (Ćulum) 1909 – 1988

**Nana passed away in 1987 after** suffering the cruel effects of senile dementia for the previous three years. Dementia is a terrible thing to happen to someone. I recall she gradually regressed from woman to child prior to her death. Towards the end she was solely dependant on those around her, especially Granddad, whose life had become that of carer, nurse and almost parent to the woman he loved.

The illness finally took its toll whilst she was in hospital after suffering a broken leg. This was the final straw her ravaged body could not handle and she sadly passed away, oblivious to the loved ones around her.

I remember going straight to Granddad after she had died, how he had cried as I placed my arms around him. Never before had I seen him cry and it hurt me so much to witness his pain.

Nana Alice, like most of her generation, had been born into a life of poverty and hardship. Her father was employed as a coal miner at Ledston Luck Colliery near the mining town of Castleford. 'Luck' had obviously not rubbed off onto her family's life; Nana's father was killed, crushed by a rock fall as he laboured, when she was still just a small child.

I would spend countless hours sitting with Nana whilst Granddad was working or tending his precious allotment. She would tell me stories from her own youth; fond memories of travelling to school by horse and cart and being sent into service, working as a maid for the local aristocrats. She would relive the war years, making ammunition and bombs at the armaments factory at Thorpe Arch in North Yorkshire. Even after the passing of so many years, her eyes would still fill with tears as she recalled the untimely death of the father she adored so much.

That day had begun like any other. She had woken early and travelled to school with the other local children where lessons were recorded on grey slate and chalk, this being a time before mass-produced and affordable paper and ink.

Horror and shock met her on her return to the family home. Instead of the freshly baked bread and homemade preserves set out on the kitchen table, there lay the bloody and lifeless body of her father. Elderly local women were busy cleaning the shattered corpse in readiness for the traditionally simple coffin of a working man.

Long before the days of the National Health Service and any sort of corporate responsibility or compassion, the bodies of miners killed on the job were simply returned to their families. Of no use now to the machinery of industrial profit, they were simply discarded and before their blood was even dry, the gap they left would be filled by fresh-faced teenagers, eager to earn a pittance in order to survive.

Nana's early life did not improve. She had married young, taken in by the charms of a local man who desired profit more than passion. With the added responsibility of children, Nana's husband took the easy option. Without remorse, he bade his family a final farewell, leaving them to their fate for the love of a younger woman.

Despite this, or perhaps because of it, she would always smile with deep pride whenever she recounted her life with the man she spent the rest of her life with, my grandfather. She had been working, after the war, at the Miners' Hostel in Castleford. Initially these hostels had been used to accommodate the influx of conscripted boys and men replacing local miners who had been sent to fight the war. With the ceasefire of hostilities in 1945, the hostels were kept in use, now used as housing for the refugees arriving in Britain from war-ravaged Europe. With the armaments factories ceasing production, Nana obtained work at the hostel and, in 1947, met Granddad for the first time.

Instant chemistry must have connected the two as, soon after, they moved into a rented house on the outskirts of Castleford. In the end, the need for a British passport, as opposed to true love and companionship, did not even enter the equation. Granddad refused citizenship and went to the grave as a Yugoslavian.

Nana would always say her life had never been a happy one until she found true love and contentment with this man who's past she knew little about, feelings proven to be carried deeply within both of them as dementia took its cruel hold over her and Granddad mourned the woman she was whilst caring for the child she became.

When Nana finally passed the house I had loved and cherished became silent. Life continued but all was not well. A huge gaping hole had been torn from the very fabric of all I had ever known.

My Nana was gone. Never again would I stand behind her chair, combing her short grey hair with brush and water in a childish attempt to straighten her natural curls. No more would I hold out my hands to accept pressed linen from the two rollers above the simple washing machine as I helped her with the household chores.

Now even the fireside people had deserted me. The invisible souls that had made the dough rise beside the warming heat of the Yorkshire Range oven had bade their final farewell. The magical earthenware pot had given up the ghost, no longer providing the very basics of nurture. Now yeast was substituted with compost, the hard working pot now a decorative object, still holding delicate summer blooms in Mam's garden to this day.

Despite his heavy loss, Granddad put on a brave face and, outwardly at least, appeared fine. Looking at him, I would often think that life could deal the cruellest of blows. To have the dearest and most precious thing on this earth taken from you just once is a terrible thing. To have it happen twice is unimaginable.

I would visit him every day to keep him company, walking the couple of miles from the house I had bought following the birth of my daughter Sasha.

He became fixated with chopping firewood in preparation for the coming winter despite it being highly unlikely he would run out of fuel. All miners received a free fuel allowance that continued after retirement.

Soon, the cellar beneath the house was full of chopped wood but still he continued, filling plastic sacks and storing them in the brick shed outside.

Maybe, with hindsight, this was a clear indication all was not as well with Granddad as we'd hoped and thought. Years later, when I visited Bosnia as the ice-cold grasp of another harsh winter was closing in, I would make my way through the mountains, passing houses with walls lined with firewood, almost as high as their roofs, displaying a similarly feverish attempt to bay back the elements as I had seen back home, from him.

Grief manifests itself in many ways and only now can I see that Granddad, without the love of his life, was simply regressing to an earlier existence he had known and cherished.

Within months of Nana's passing, he began complaining of pain in his back, totally out of character for him. I had never known him complain of any illness or ailment. Even when it was obvious he was unwell, he would never say a word.

He started to eat very little, and when he did he was violently sick. Hours were spent sat in front of the old heat lamp bought to ease the pain of an earlier spinal injury.

Eventually, he was persuaded to seek medical advice and was referred to the local hospital. X-rays confirmed he had an abnormality on one lung. Further tests, using a camera inserted down his throat, diagnosed he had a cancerous growth on his stomach. It was terminal.

In that one word my entire world was blown apart. I remember walking with no particular direction or destination, just walking, lost.

I have since read that it is a very fine rope we walk between sanity and insanity; one wrong step could make all the difference. Looking back, I now see I had at this moment, taken this wrong step, and was spiralling headfirst into a mental breakdown.

Like most faced with impending loss, I convinced myself everyone was wrong and that I was right. The man would never die; he was naturally immortal. He was untouchable and would always be there for me, the closest friend I would ever have, and most of all, as he was so very different and unique, unlike anyone else I had known, something as monotonous as cancer could not be the end of him.

He was and would forever be the foreign freedom fighter that I became when playing out fantasies of past battles in the streets as a child.

Whenever I wasn't working, I would get hopelessly drunk and in the early hours, leave the house and walk to nowhere, lost in my own intoxicated thoughts.

It was July when the doctors said he had just a matter of months to live. He would not see the following Christmas. Cancer is the cruellest of diseases and I watched hopelessly as it quickly took its toll. The giant was dwindling before my very eyes; the brightest of gazes was flickering like that of a candle which had burned through the night.

The following months remain a blur, a lost segment of my life. I would visit him daily – religiously - either at his home or the hospital. The fixation with stockpiling fuel intensified. I attempted to appease this and would fill a wheelbarrow with coal from my own stock, wearily pushing this to add to the growing pile within the cellar.

Christmas approached and Mam wanted him to come home from his latest stint in hospital to spend what would be his last Christmas with the people he loved around him, in surroundings he knew. The consultants responsible for the care of this dying man prescribed a heavy dose of steroids before Granddad was finally released. The senior doctor warned us that we should not allow appearances to be deceptive. The man we loved had already crossed the line into death and the medication would only offer us a glimpse of what he had once been.

Whatever drugs had been pumped into his bloodstream seemed to me to be a miracle cure. The unbeatable giant had once again risen from his deathbed. As if by magic, the emaciated face reminiscent of a concentration camp victim was once again plump and filled with colour and life. The beard however, would have to go I thought!

That Christmas Day will stay ingrained in my memory for the rest of my life. I remember every minute detail as if it was yesterday; from what we ate to the clothes we wore. As usual, Granddad joined in with the festivities. The obligatory paper hat was worn and the dried out turkey was eaten. We tried hard not to dwell too much on Nana's empty chair and the passing year was toasted with cheap wine and light festivities.

With Christmas gone his condition quickly worsened and soon he was bedridden. The magical steroids had run their course just as the doctor predicted. With no other choice, he was admitted to Ackton Hospital on the fringes of

Featherstone. The hospital had originally been commissioned as a contagious disease isolation building but had now become a 'do or die' hospital. Patients were either admitted to convalesce or to finally meet their maker. Unfortunately for Granddad, his fate laid with the latter.

It was whilst there his cancer took its cruellest turn. It had spread to his brain and caused him to relive and re-enact scenes from his previous life in Yugoslavia. He would be fighting in the mountains and speak of leading men through Bosnia to the safety of the allies in liberated Italy. He rarely spoke English now and when we visited him, we would take a close friend of his to act as an interpreter.

At times he would fly into wild rages. I remember being so frightened whenever this happened because I had never seen the man angry before. He would sit upright in bed, startled from sleep, and draw his finger across his throat in a gestured threat whilst shouting orders to unseen fighters. Most of my visiting time would be spent apologising to startled companions of other dearly loved ones, who were now facing death themselves.

His condition worsened and it was decided he should be placed into a single, private room, away from the main ward. He now barely woke from his morphine-induced slumber, and on the morning of March 17$^{th}$ 1988, his final fight for freedom came to an end as he quietly passed away.

I will never forget the utter feeling of desolation as my parents solemnly broke the news that Maksim had fought his very last battle. In the end, it was cancer which had triumphed where so many others had failed, over forty years later.

I simply stared at their saddened faces. I waited for the punch line to a joke never to materialise. There had to be some mistake, I still could not accept what had been inevitable from the very beginning.

Maksim had gone. Maximus, as I fondly saw him, had fought his final gladiatorial battle. First his body wasted and then he died. He had not died a hero's death, but had simply surrendered, piece by piece, as the cancer ravaged his body and his very soul conceded defeat, accepting its final fate.

The man was gone. Friend, hero, teacher had now left me forever. The following weeks went by in a complete blur. I vaguely remember attending the sombre funeral and that the Vicar had made the event as Orthodox as he possibly could, given he was himself Church of England. The same holy man who had drunk a toast of whisky with Granddad was now committing his body to the ground.

I can still see clearly in my mind's eye, the grief-laden sobs of Mam as she read the simple card I had embedded in a bouquet of flowers. Simply, it read, "To the best friend I have ever had, and could ever have."

It was so ironic that at the cemetery, I noticed for the first time, the burial plot Nana already occupied was directly backing onto Granddad's closest friend. Milan had died prematurely, some seven years prior. So close in life, they would now rest head to head for eternity.

As the all-consuming grief slowly eased a little, I found the courage to enter Granddad's house. A place once was filled with so many living memories was now cold and empty. In every room I entered, I expected him to be there wearing the smile could melt even the hardest heart etched upon his face in simple greeting.

He was not, and never would be there again, it slowly dawned on me, as I took in the atmosphere of the house for the very last time, straining to commit every corner to memory as I looked through tear filled eyes.

Mam had told me whatever I wanted from the house was mine to take. Materialistic things, however, can never be a substitute for loss, and I cupped in my hands the only item that meant so much to me - a deeply engraved pocket watch I had bought him as a gift some six years prior.

As I held the watch in the empty room, I was taken back to the day I'd handed him the gift with deep-rooted pride. Nana and Granddad had given me so much in life. Now, it was my turn, as a waged man, to return the favour. At just sixteen years of age, I was finally the man I had always been destined to be. Old King Coal had called to me and I had eagerly followed him into the bowels of the earth. I now desperately felt the desire to give back a little something to the people I loved dearly.

Like all coal mines of the time, Sharlston Colliery offered its workforce the chance to purchase goods; the price would then be deducted each week from their wages until the full cost had been recovered. This offered the working man the chance to purchase luxury items without his family having to forfeit any of life's essentials.

For Mam, I chose a brass miners' lamp. Unlike the ones offered for sale in the local shops, the ones from the colliery were exactly the same as those used to detect any presence of gas underground. At the time, these lamps were fashionable and would be displayed on the hearths of traditional coal-burning fireplaces.

The watch had caught my eye as I scanned the offerings before me. The engraved stag, leaping through the undergrowth of some unknown mountain scene, seemed perfect and was purchased without any thought of cost.

As I stood alone within the surroundings I cherished, I felt warmth filling the room from the coal-fired stove. I could smell the aroma of fresh bread and lamb stew, simmering away gently.

Nana sat in her floral patterned chair, nearest the glowing coals of the fire, her silver hair still damp. Granddad sat opposite on the sofa.

"Andre," (he never pronounced the w) he said, as I stepped into the room. I walked over and placed the box in front of him on the small table.

"What's this?" he asked, looking at the box. I remember as if it were yesterday, the warm glow spreading across his face as he slowly drew the watch from its box, running his fingertips over the engraved scene of a deer in woodland.

With the warmest of smiles he looked at me and cupped his huge hands over the watch, holding it up near his left cheek and in this moment the illusion is gone and tears of deep grief snatch me from my memory as I look down at the same watch, in the same room now cold without the warming glow of the fire. The furniture remained, but I now stood alone with nothing but my grief for company.

Without even a final glance, I turned quickly and left the room, still clutching the watch that would remain my companion for the next twenty years.

Even today, the feelings of being cheated out of more time with my mentor remain embedded in my very soul. So many questions remain unanswered and I still feel the guilt he plainly carried within him and the hopelessness he felt at never being able to tell his own story. How he must have sat alone at night with his burden, carried without relief.

People all around him, but feeling so very alone, an island cut off by his own thoughts and memories. Maybe he thought he had to protect us. Maybe his mind had simply locked it all away, but in hiding the life of love, happiness and abject horror he had known in Yugoslavia he had, so far, been successful.

\* \* \* \*

# Displaced
## Our Lives So Differently Told

## Chapter Four - The Beginning of the End

**With his death, Granddad had become** a closed book. The pages of Maksim Ćulumović were now sealed, with no further chance for anyone to peruse the pages. It was as if the book had simply never existed.

The initial shock gradually faded and was replaced by the desperate and all-consuming feeling of loneliness. Although family and friends surrounded me, I felt, for the very first time in my life, so very alone and isolated.

My rock had gone and I felt myself drifting into my thoughts more and more. Birthdays and Christmas' were especially poignant and I would wait for the greeting cards which would never arrive. For years, I would forget just long enough to sift through the pile of envelopes and slowly have it dawn on me why it was a fruitless task. Those happy times with my grandparents were behind me now.

Regrets; I held many in the coming months, but the greatest is the inspiration for the text you are reading now.

Sometime, in early 1984, Granddad expressed the thought that he should write a book. This shocked me, as he had been so illusive with any information about his past, it seemed out of character to consider writing of it.

I asked what the title of the book would be.

"Displaced Persons," he simply replied, "the contents would be of interest to all who would read the pages of my life".

Looking back, I was so foolish to brush this to one side without much thought. It is especially hard to think of this random comment now after pursuing his story across land and sea, looking for the truth that may have once come from the man himself.

Unfortunately, at the time, I was fighting for my own beliefs and livelihood. I was caught up in the bitter, year-long miners' strike gripping the nation. The strike passed with countless stories told of the political struggle. Instead, I frittered away twelve months chasing a dream. As a united force, the miners could once again overthrow the government as they had ten years before.

Naivety and a deep-rooted passion to save Britain's industrial heritage, blinded me and tens of thousands of other striking miners. We thought we would be victorious like our fathers before us. Instead, we were defeated by a government hell bent on seeking revenge. The miners would be beaten at all cost; mining villages were to be sealed off by the deployment of a police force that seemed to grow from nowhere. Families were starved without pity and 'snatch squads' of heavily armoured invaders would put as many of the strikers under lock and key as they could. Death, severe beatings and malnutrition became too much of a burden to bear. In March 1985 the National Union of Mineworkers' leadership urged the most militant of us to return to work.

With heads held high, even in defeat, thousands of us marched back through colliery gates. Traditional colliery brass bands led the way. Despite the music, however, each and every one of us knew the end was nigh.

Despite being retired from the mines Granddad had been against the strike. Not that he thought the working man deserved better, but because he suspected the unions leadership of being driven by communist ideology. Arthur Scargill, the mineworker's national leader to me was a class hero. Unfortunately to Granddad he was the 'enemy within'. Old beliefs they say never die. Long debates regarding politics would take place between the two of us over games of chess.

"Be a leader, not the follower," he would always announce as his proud Bishop proclaimed the final check mate of my never ending defeat.

Colliery after colliery was closed and finally, in 1993, the most profitable of the mines were finally sealed in a last, vicious blow by a vengeful government. In ten years, over two hundred thousand coal miners lost their jobs and a large piece of the 'Great' became wiped from Britain's name forever.

How very sad that I did not take up the challenge to tell the man's story as he had wished. Maybe then I would not have been consumed by my desire to pick out the fragments of his life, in order to put them into their final print.

In the summer of Granddad's death, my parents decided to take a holiday in the Adriatic resort of Makarska, now part of independent Croatia. This was not unusual, as they had travelled to Yugoslavia before, chasing the dream of a relatively cheap holiday, compared to France and Spain.

On their return, they visited me with the usual duty free cigarettes and tobacco. I was told they had attempted to find the illusive village of Granddad's birth, to retrieve some of its native soil to spread on his final resting place.

The good friend acting as interpreter at Granddad's deathbed, had, to some degree, finally broken the code of silence. He gave the name of Granddad's birth village, writing it in Serbian Latin on a scrap of paper.

My parents hired a car for the day and set off, trying to follow the forty year-old directions given to them. After perhaps eight hours of driving through rugged terrain, they stumbled, more by accident than skilful navigation, on a place Mam recognised from one of Granddad's talks to her as a child.

The village appeared quite dilapidated, and was approached by driving over a shallow stream lined with old timbers. One of the first buildings they encountered, and the largest, was that of a store and makeshift bar combined. They slowed to a halt opposite and showed an elderly resident the piece of paper with Granddad's details and their intended destination. The man glanced at the paper and appeared to show little interest before turning and carrying on with his chore.

Moving steadily onwards into the small hamlet, they again drew slowly to a stop where a group of locals were whiling the day away with idle banter. Again, they were beckoned to look at the offered piece of paper, and again, their response was that of disinterest, even slight disapproval, before returning to their conversation.

Mam recalls feeling as if their presence in the village was being scrutinised and questioned in the fast pace of the locals' banter.

One elderly gentleman, however, left the group and approached the car once more. He motioned to be shown the paper again. After slowly scrutinising it, he pointed towards the track that led to the last of the dwellings. With two upturned fingers, he motioned that once they reached these buildings they should walk in the pointed direction.

With a most nervous 'thank you' they drove the car the twenty or so metres to the last of the village buildings, drawing to a halt as the track slowly gave way to thick grass before being lost from sight altogether.

Turning off the ignition and opening the car doors, they were immediately met by an approaching police officer, from the direction of the group of locals with whom they had spoken just moments earlier.

On first impressions it was obvious the officer was not a happy man. On second impressions, given the fact he had drawn his firearm, it was obvious he was maybe even a little bit angry.

The sight of a gun and a lack of understanding of its bearer's language, Mam recalls can be quite chilling to say the least. She remembers having the feeling that she was about to die hundreds of miles from home, in a place she did not know. (I myself would momentarily experience the same feelings of dread, some twenty years later, in my own quest to find the same illusive village).

She recalls, instinctively, her arms rose above her head in surrender, like a captured fugitive from some Hollywood movie. Thankfully, this seemed to calm the explosive situation, and the officer sheathed his gun in the holster at his waist.

No sooner had this happened than a car came towards them from the direction of the village and two plain-clothed men climbed from its interior. After exchanging the briefest of acknowledgement with the officer, the two men took charge of the situation.

In between silent prayers, Mam recalls pushing her memory to its limit, trying to remember anything Granddad had told her which may diffuse the situation. As a child, she had helped him learn the English language, but in return had learnt little, if any, of his native tongue. One of his close friends had taught her a phrase to shout out, but luckily she remembered Granddads reaction to this phrase being less than favourable to say the least and decided not to recite what she had learnt. I discovered years later that saying, "Shut up, stupid Bosnian," would not have been a wise move given their interrogators were armed.

She recalls Granddad always told her as a child of how he loved to swim, and not too far from where he had lived there was a beautiful river and lake. Now she was faced with a problem. He would speak of Pliva and Pivo; she remembered one was a river, the other a brand of beer. Which was which; unfortunately, she could not remember.

Luckily, her gamble paid off, as she said "Pliva" to the interrogators, lowering her hand to shade her eyes, in gesture of scanning the horizon. Pliva is a river in that part of Bosnia. Imagine the explaining she would have had to do had she chosen the other, saying: "I am here, looking for beer!"

Not entirely satisfied, their interrogators gestured the motions of swimming and bathing costumes, prodding at father's clothing as if to prompt him to reveal that underneath he was indeed equipped for a marathon swim.

With no bathing costume offered, the attention was directed towards the rental car and, although barriers to language were strong, Mam recalls it being obvious accusations were being made that the car had been stolen.

Maybe the three wise men had uncovered two of Europe's most evil of villains who had neither entered the village to swim in Pliva - or drink Pivo - but were there for underworld activities unknown to them, or...perhaps not. Whatever the reason for the harsh treatment, (still unknown to this day), the experience shocked Mam badly, and it was to be another nineteen years before she would set foot on Yugoslav soil again.

With no evidence to hold my parents further, the officials gestured for them to get back into the hire car and follow their vehicle. They directed my parents onto a road heading south away from the village and with no other choice, they followed their new directions.

On returning to England, my parents wrote to the Yugoslavian Embassy in London about the treatment they had received. A reply followed within the week and the only explanation offered was that they had caused a great deal of curiosity in the area during their short-lived visit. Staff at the Embassy apologised for their mistreatment and said they were more than welcome to visit Yugoslavia again in the future.

Whatever had been written on the piece of paper I will never know. Mam, still frightened by the ordeal, destroyed it during the long drive back to Makarska. .

The following years saw little, or no progress in my search. Letters to the Embassy in Belgrade proved fruitless, with no information offered about any Maksim Ćulumović. At times I would even question myself whether or not the man had ever existed.

What made matters even worse was the spelling of the name. As a child, Mam had recalled seeing the name written with two different spellings, Ćulumović and Čulumovic. Although to my eyes, the difference was negligible; I would be informed years later this difference was a significant factor when tracing a family name. The spelling of Čulumovic was very rare indeed. So rare, in fact, it would be highly likely that anyone with the name spelt in this particular way would be related to one another.

Unfortunately, catastrophic events unfolded in Yugoslavia in the early 1990s, with the country plunging into civil war. Slovenia and Macedonia broke away and became independent countries. Croatia attempted to follow their lead, but was met with stiff resistance from the Yugoslavian Government. Fighting soon broke out and an all out civil war ensued.

Bosnia also claimed independence, igniting the age-old hatred between Serbia and Croatia. Both sides saw Bosnia as theirs and bloody conflict erupted.

British television was filled with scenes of utter horror and carnage. As the months slowly passed, a vile terror was unleashed as the conflict consumed Bosnia.

I remember being drawn to the horrific media coverage and how I would become emotional for reasons unclear to me.

Until then, I had been led to believe Granddad had been Serbian and had lived his early life in Serbia. He had only ever mentioned Bosnia just prior to his death whilst reliving events from World War Two.

I recall the feelings of hatred I felt for the people responsible on all sides of the conflict for their acts of murder and savagery. I felt deeply saddened for a country I had only visited in my imagination. My determination to seek out the truth was fuelled by every vicious act portrayed on screen and I found myself drawn even further towards the country and its people.

A magnetic pull reached out and took hold, enveloping me in its grasp never to let go.

\* \* \* \*

# Displaced

## Our Lives So Differently Told

## Chapter Five - Is There Anybody Out There?

**People say grieving is a slow** progress only time can heal. Just as you start to become used to the loss of a loved one, you fleetingly catch their reflection in the corner of your eye, turn to look closer and realise they are gone, that they were never really there.

Maybe grief never leaves us at all and we cope with the loss rather than forget. Looking back on all the years I've searched, it's more than probable that with every scrap of information I gleaned I was keeping the man alive in my own heart, feeling the need to remain connected to him, to bridge the divide between life and death.

With his passing, a void was created within my soul. Searching for anything connected with him always felt like a small part of me was in his presence, connected with him long after his death.

I had been given a taste, but only that, of people so different to those I was accustomed. Now I had become hungry and wanted to know more, everything. I visualised a place so beautiful and serene, a place only written about in books and depicted in pictures taken long ago.

I would dream of walking through a place filled with long grass blowing softly in the cool breeze, stepping into the footprints of the man that had walked there so many years before.

I would hear laughter and gaze at a child who would shout for it's mam, wanting to be fed from the breast so eagerly, but then, as always, the breeze would die and the grass and the dream would falter. Grief would creep out from it's momentary hiding place and the reality of my loss would crash over me like an unstoppable tidal wave.

Some say the internet is a curse created by mankind. Others say it is one of the wonders of the modern world. My own introduction to this powerful tool came belatedly, but it was invaluable in helping me on my journey to Bosnia and ultimately, Granddad.

My search was amplified with the information now at my fingertips and I would spend hours each day typing in the very basic information I had.

Name, Date of Birth, Nationality. I had one photograph of a uniformed man, a brass military cap badge, two gold and mother of pearl tunic cuff buttons and a photograph of King Petar II Karađorđević, Yugoslavia's last king before the outbreak of World War Two.

Genealogy in the UK has become big business, with everyone wanting to find their roots. Maybe we search in the hope of discovering unknown riches or perhaps it's simple curiosity or lost connections to once cherished family members.

Whatever the cause, it seems the interest has gone global as I found a website devoted to Serbian Genealogy. Maybe I expected too much, but I received little. Despite posting for Ćulumović or Čulumovic, there came nothing in the way of information. People there were friendly and it became obvious they wanted to help but could offer no information with the name I searched.

I continued to post on the forum with utter determination, each scrap of evidence would be sent with the eternal hope that someone, somewhere, would make the connection, and finally give me the answers I so desperately searched for.

Mam recalled the village of her mistreatment as being something akin to the pronunciation of Briani and again this information was posted on the website's forum. Two photographs had been written on in a foreign tongue with a faint hand and were now carefully translated for me by readers of the forum.

The first photograph, translated using the Cry1llic alphabet, depicted two women and a teenage girl, all looking quite sombre and dressed in dark clothing. It bore the text:

"To Maksim, reminiscing and long remembering from your wife and daughter Zorka and niece Milka, lot of respect Stojana."

The second photograph, written in the Latin alphabet, portrayed two women, three young girls and a boy. This inscription read:

"To my son-in-law, Maksim Ćulumović, with greetings from Liubica, Stojan, Radmila, Rade, Violeta and Budimir, 27/02/1949, Bijelo Polje, Independent State of Montenegro."

One of the women in that photograph was almost identical in appearance to the wife, Stojana, in the first picture.

Although Granddad always maintained his family were dead, Mam recalls how, as a child, she would, in fact, help him put together packages of tea and other items to send to a surviving sister-in-law.

She also recalled the anger he had shown one day on discovering the sister-in-law had married a communist. Whatever the reason and the full story, she could not recall hearing of any further communication between the pair after this announcement.

Mam also remembers seeing the picture of the three women and, as children often do, she laughed at their appearance. The people pictured were rather stern-looking individuals to say the least, dressed not for the swinging 60s, but more akin to people suffering the hardship that follows warfare.

She recalls Granddad hurriedly putting the picture into his pocket and scorning her severely for laughing at his wife. Mam never saw the photograph again until after his death when the forbidden suitcase was opened one last time.

Armed with the information the photographs offered I was finally able to focus my search on an actual place. Montenegro was my next target.

Research showed that this surely was the connection I had been searching for. Bijelo Polje actually existed and, for the next six months, all of my attention was drawn there.

A place of beauty - nestled within the eye-catching scenery of rolling, forest-covered hills and mountains, it created a stunning image that could easily have been snatched from any traditional children's fairy tale book.

Once again, armed with this new information, I spent hours corresponding on both Serbian and Montenegrin forums with little to no success. Ćulumović was not a native name there and I soon discovered from the many people I spoke with that it was unheard of in the region.

With every week the hope that the information I held was enough to uncover the truth died a little more, until the stark realisation came, at least where Bijelo Polje was concerned, I would find no answers. Appeals were broadcast on Radio Bijelo Polje but no one came forward with any information to help my search. It seemed that with Maksim a closed book, the true identities of the people captured in the photographs would be forever lost within those pages.

Historians, experts in the field of Balkan history, urged me not to give up. Post-war Yugoslavia had been a hive of activity, with the newly installed socialist government relocating vast swathes of refugees, displaced through four years of occupation and civil war. Bijelo Polje may have merely been a temporary, transitional stop for the people in the photographs.

I would look endlessly at the two images and imagine these people in real life, trying to beckon them into my reality and beg answers to my questions.

It was a cruel game, peering at these people, but having no sense of the essence of their being, their memories and knowledge, their stories. Without that piece of the puzzle, that additional information, a photograph is useless and only acts as a tantalising glimpse of life, which tortures and invokes despair if you try and read past its aesthetic appeal.

Whenever I look at those two photographs, my mind is cast back to my own childhood and how different our lives must have been.

Granddad, I now see, was also living the life he had dreamt of during his years in England. Although he appeared happy with our way of life, I now realise just how alienated and alone he must have felt.

He was not just being "different and stubborn" as people often remarked, but was merely continuing his true self in an environment to which he was not accustomed, and could never fully adjust to.

Maybe, just maybe, this is the reason for my own extensive, never-ending search. My attempt to reinstate in my life whatever it was that Granddad had lost forever in his.

Perhaps, the poor tomato boy with the wheelbarrow was purposefully ingrained into me, as was the lone soldier on the battlegrounds of Featherstone. However it had happened, as I had grown, so had the urge to uncover the truth, once and for all.

Bijelo Polje and Montenegro held whatever secrets they had firmly to their chest and offered no fragment of hope for me in my search. This, I found, was to be the first of countless frustrations I would encounter over the coming years. For the first time I had images of real people and a real place and I knew it. I wasn't going to give up.

Looking back, maybe I was not yet prepared to face the enormity of what it was I sought. The feelings of frustration and fading hopes continued with every step forward I made, causing me to arrive at an abrupt stop before starting over once again.

The Yugoslavian forums suggested my search could have links to the Lika area of Croatia. There was a place resembling Mam's recollections of the pronunciation of her visit. She spoke of Briani; posts to the forum suggested Brianne and this place lay to the west of Pliva National Park.

This was finally, I thought, the connection without doubt, another actual place - and a direct link to the word 'Pliva' as well as to Granddad. 'Pliva', he would recall fondly from the days of his youth, with tales of how he would swim in the rivers and waterfalls.

The National Park of Pliva is truly a place of outstanding beauty. Unspoilt, idyllic mountain slopes, interspersed with continuous cascades of crystal-clear water, thundering their way down from the mountainous confines before finally coming to rest within the depths of the Adriatic Sea.

With renewed determination, I explored every possibility this place offered, scrutinising every aspect of it and making as many links as I could, however tenuous, desperate for that one lead which would unveil the truth, but as the months spent researching raced by with no concrete results, my hope dwindled. Ćulumović families had been known in the area, but after correspondence, none of the families recognised the name 'Maksim' or any of the people depicted in the photographs.

Again, I was drawn to the stark possibility that the man of my search had never existed. I was now becoming convinced, as I had suspected from the beginning, that his identity had been changed and, quite possibly, my questions would never be answered.

With every setback came the memories of the man that was my grandfather. I would be drawn back to simpler times in my life, times I felt secure and at ease, days filled with happiness and contentment.

I always recall the warmth I felt whenever I was in the presence of Granddad and the security this feeling gave me.

My thoughts would drift back to my school years, where I would call at my grandparent's house to make sure their buckets of coal were full enough to last until my return later in the afternoon and how it never felt like a chore that *had* to be done.

I always remember in particular, two days each year when there would be a crudely baked circle of bread placed on the table with a lone candle burning brightly in its centre. I would rush home from school, all adolescent eagerness to see if the candle still burned. It always did, just as brightly as it did earlier in the day and would continue to do so well into the night. Maturity and age often spoil the show and give a rational explanation to our childhood memories of happiness and innocence. Looking back now, the eternal candle had not been a gift from the gods, as I believed, but was merely replaced in my absence. Sometimes, it is so nice to be naïve and open to suggestion.

I remember too, the merriment which always followed the setting of the sun. The table would be full of the most beautiful foods - cold hams, freshly baked breads, cheeses and potatoes and drink flowed freely throughout, as if there was a never-ending supply. The older generations, fuelled by its effect, would proceed to make attempts at a strange dance, a dance their aged bodies could no longer accomplish with anything resembling style or grace.

My childish self would still be drawn to the burning bread that had retained its fire for so long, and I would ask, with hungry anticipation, if this too could be eaten.

"No!" was always the disappointing reply; this was being saved for the saints.

Granddad would say the celebrations were his "Glory Day" but would never elaborate further.

Since my search I have found he was, in fact, celebrating the family Slava, a custom he continued until his death. (Slava is the Orthodox Christian Custom of honouring a family patron saint. It is traditionally celebrated by the Serbs.)

I have since discovered Granddad's saint had been George - the same dragon-slaying Saint George who is celebrated in England. He would, however, celebrate St George's day on May 6th, rather than the traditional English day of April 23rd. The reason for this, I learnt, was that he continued to use the traditional Julian calendar of his lost homeland.

Unusually he also celebrated another Slava, or Glory Day in November. This puzzled me as tradition was for each family to celebrate one Saint. To have two was very unusual. I would learn later in some cases it was customary to celebrate a Saint's day close to some catastrophic event. November had been the month is world had been shattered with the merciless butchering of his family and friends. Maybe the second Slava had been his private way of remembrance.

What appeared to be the first of genuine breakthrough came for me in the spring of 2007 by the way of my Mam's invitation for me to meet with one of the last of the surviving

Yugoslavians that had arrived in the UK following their exodus from post-war Yugoslavia.

Bob Krlic was the young cousin of Granddad's friend Milan and was now maybe in his late seventies. Mam had remembered him visiting Granddad on many occasions when she had been a child. It was hoped he could shed some light on the mystery once and for all.

Armed, like the most intrepid of explorers, with all the information I had, I visited him with my parents. Photographs, maps, papers, all gathered together with my hope this lead would not be a dead end like all of those that came before it.

I was made most welcome with the offer of coffee and cakes and felt comfortable in the man's company as well as his wife's, Boja. I would see this kind of hospitality repeated within the next two years whenever I was invited into strangers' homes during my visits to Bosnia.

Mam had not seen the man since her early years and much of the meeting was spent reminiscing and telling catch up stories to bridge the slightly awkward gap which grows with the passing of time.

I handed Bob the patchy information I had gleaned painstakingly over the years and waited for his response.

I remember him leafing through the notes I had made. Quite strangely, he expressed his concerns that maybe I should stop the search immediately. I asked why and he simply said the place of my search was now occupied by the Muslim faith and I would find nothing there to help me.

Vividly, I recall, as he turned over the photograph of the uniformed Maksim,

"Chulum!" He called out - as if by instinct.

Even more so, I recall his wife's response as he voiced the name; she rose from her chair and harshly corrected him,

"That this was not his name!" Boja corrected harshly.

Bob retreated immediately and shrugged saying Chulum was just the nickname he had known him as.

Little, if any, information was gleaned from this meeting and I came away with scantily more than I had set out with.

It was like encountering a code of silence which had remained in place since the displaced refugees had arrived in the UK. Whatever their reasons, it seemed no one was willing to breach this confidence regardless of the time that has passed.

Two things had come out of the encounter though - Muslims and the name Chulum. The latter I would, to my detriment, ignore for the next twelve months.

I had become knowledgeable enough to realise the Muslim faith was closely connected to Bosnia but had never imagined this was the place that my search should focus. In fact, within what was formerly Yugoslavia, this would have been the last place I envisioned. Granddad had been secretive, yes, but not once had I heard him mention, in the slightest, any connection to Bosnia that was not a fleeting military reference.

* * * *

# Displaced

## Our Lives So Differently Told

# Chapter Six - Bosnia Old Country of Scars

**Bosnia is home to three ethnic** "constituent peoples". Bosniaks represent the largest population group, Serbs the second largest and Croats the third. Regardless of ethnicity, a citizen of Bosnia and Herzegovina is often identified in English as a Bosnian. In Bosnia itself, the distinction between a Bosnian and a Herzegovinian is maintained as a regional, rather than an ethnic distinction. The country is politically decentralised and comprises two governing entities: the Federation of Bosnia and Herzegovina and Republika Srspska. Formerly one of the six federal units constituting Yugoslavia, Bosnia and Herzegovina gained its independence during the Yugoslav Civil Wars of the 1990s. Bosnia and Herzegovina can be described as a Federal Democratic Republic that is transforming its economy into a market-oriented system and it is a potential candidate for joining the European Union.

Since the meeting with the surviving Yugoslav refugee, I spent the following months scanning Google Earth ™ satellite images of Bosnia and searched online for any maps that were available.

Numerous emails were sent to the Yugoslavian Combatants Organisation in London requesting any information they could offer. Each day I would open my inbox, waiting for a reply which would never come.

Out of sheer desperation, I contacted a private genealogical investigator based in Montenegro and gave her all the information I had. Quickly, she got to work and spoke to most, if not all, Ćulumović families in Bosnia.

Although the usual response was of pleasure that interest was being shown to trace lost people, the answer was always the same, none had any known connection to the name 'Maksim' in their family history.

Months of searching online photographs finally paid off however, when I discovered another photo of Maksim. Research revealed that the photograph was taken near to the town of Čakac, Serbia, and depicted men from the Yugoslavian army. Granddad, as in the earlier photograph, was pictured laying down at the front; either he was an extremely lazy man or the placement, always in a prone position, was that of seniority. This stance would continue in later photographs after he had arrived in England. Each group photograph taken shows him in exactly the same position, lying down at the foot of the group as if his image had been superimposed onto the picture.

I once asked a work colleague to look at the photographs and tell me their interpretation of Granddad's prone position. With a wry smile she quick-wittedly announced 'maybe he was merely lazy and enjoyed a rest!'

During this time a strange thing happened. Prior to his death, I recalled seeing resettlement documents he had kept locked away in the old suitcase. I searched the house countless times, but these papers constantly alluded me. I thought they must have been accidentally and tragically, lost over the years.

Whilst looking for something unrelated to my search, I opened a writing bureau where I kept all legal documents and papers of importance. My gaze was immediately drawn to a dishevelled, faded brown envelope lying on top of the stacks of paper.

I tipped out the envelope's contents and was shocked to see photographs of Maksim fall out before my eyes. After my initial surprise, I gathered them up and spread them carefully out onto the carpet. Not only were there photographs, but resettlement paperwork from Italy, Germany and the UK. I doubt very much this was part of some unexplained divine intervention, more likely I had overlooked the envelope in my haste to actually find it.

The papers inside were of vital importance. They recorded personal information he had never divulged, keeping secret to the end.

Name, date of birth and, more importantly, his birthplace were recorded on each document. Strangely, however, both marital status and place of birth differed for every country. Birthplace was recorded as being Brzani, Brdzani and Brdjani and marital status implied that he had been both single and widowed.

Other records and information stated he was Serbian by nationality, was of Orthodox religion and his parents were Jovo and Petra (his mother's maiden name recorded as being Lukić).

On one document it was stated his birthplace, spelt as Brdjani, was in the province of Jaljce.

Amongst the paperwork I found other documents that recorded the involvement of the police in the UK. Mam recalled, as a child, Police Officers would visit the house on a regular basis, and one time in particular, they'd visited unexpectedly and had almost discovered the illegal distillation of whisky being produced in the cellar.

These papers were of vital significance, as I had, through a close contact, police records checked with what was then the 'Aliens' Department'. No record, however, ever came back with connection to the name or address I presented. Despite the documents I had found proving otherwise, it was once again as if the man had never actually existed. There was no corresponding file for him with the authorities, yet in my hand was a record of weekly visits, signatures of the attending officers and fingerprints of the man they were, for whatever reason, monitoring closely.

I was drawn to the photographs amongst the collection of paperwork. Photographs of the man I had never known, in his youthful prime.

One in particular depicted him in full body plaster-cast, following the accident that had broken his back soon after he had commenced work underground at Fryston Colliery. Despite the pain and discomfort his smile shone through, the same smile that would warm its way through the worries and woes of my childhood. Truly this was a smile to warm a thousand hearts.

Whenever I look at that particular photograph, I am instantly transported to times past - times of sunshine and the songs of birds in the hedgerows of the allotment.

He would always be stood, naked to the waist and I would be drawn to the vivid scar running upwards along his spine. No matter how the sun darkened his skin, this mark always remained a white slash through the very centre of him.

We would sit, wherever the shade offered and he would talk of nature and its wonders; how the land, if respected, would reflect its appreciation with the fruits of its offerings, and we should need nothing else in life.

He would lose himself at times in this talk and take long pauses. I would always wait patiently for the dam of silence to break, although it never would and he would always withdraw momentarily into himself, as if to gain composure whenever he felt the talk was becoming too open, before he said something he really did not want to expose.

He would break the connection and send me to the well for water. On my return, the conversation was diverted, as if the previous debate had never taken place.

All too soon the sun diminished, the birdsong faded as if it had never chorused, the aromas withdrew and I would be sat alone, photograph in hand.

Maybe, as I look back, true displacement is never knowing. Displacement in Granddad's case was seeing both sides of the coin as it was flipped and being able to compare them. Both sides bear their own memories for comparison - the good, the bad and the horrors. Maybe it is worse to have only ever seen one side, knowing the other existed, but never seeing it with your own eyes.

The other aspect, always there; out of sight, never to turn, always just out of reach.

Armed with the information offered up by the resettlement records, I re-concentrated my search on the sketchy maps available online and posted new requests for help on the Serbian genealogy forum, Rodoslovje.

Researchers from the Serbian Genealogical Society suggested the most likely spelling of the birthplace would be Brdjani, or rather Brđani to be precise.

The way forward should have been wide open for me from that point, but villages with the name of Brdjani or Brđani, were in abundance within the territories of the former Yugoslavia. Brđani simply means 'hilly', or 'hill people'.

I found there were at least four places with this name in Serbia; three in Bosnia and one in Croatia. Again, weeks of frustration followed as I carefully pieced together what information I had.

The town of Jajce looked promising for my immediate search. This name was, in fact, a municipality in Bosnia and was unique. What's more, there was a Brdjani / Brđani settlement lying about thirty miles south-west of the town. One resettlement record had indicated that Jajce had been Granddad's last place of residence. Another paper made reference to Brđani coming under direct jurisdiction of Jajce.

Numerous postings on the online forums proved fruitless. No information, spanning a period of months, offered up anything regarding this place.

Innocently, I posted requests for help on a Bosnian forum, giving the link to a blog page I was running, and posting new information relating to my search as well as photographs of people that, at one time, had been close to Granddad.

I was shocked and saddened to experience the responses my simple request evoked.

In the safety of our armchairs we never fully take on board the news images filtering through to us from areas of the world embroiled in deadly conflict.

We see only what the authorities deign fit for our viewing. The images are carefully constructed and staged in a manner which is meticulously rehearsed; a diluted glimpse, never giving us a true picture of what may be happening.

When fresh news breaks to the surface, yesterday's stories are pushed to the back of our minds and we take on the wrong assumption that previous conflicts are now settled. Yesterday's footage of horror, replaced with that of peace and harmony or more likely, carnage elsewhere in the world.

This was my first time during the whole of my search I encountered the fact that not everything was settled in Bosnia. Age-old beliefs and divisions were still high on the agenda, and deep-rooted suspicions of answering questions were now to block my search.

People simply did not wish to offer any information for fear remembrance would awaken divisions which had been simmering just below the surface for countless years. I have no doubt that a similar search today would encounter the same road blocks.

Within days I came to the conclusion the forums would not offer me the magical answers I so desperately sought. I would have to proceed again, on my own, without the vital help I needed from the people that could have held the golden key. The lock I craved to open would, at this rate, remain closed tight.

Not only were people cautious with their response to forum posts, on one particular forum my requests for information were met with open hostility and threats of violence if I was to ever set foot on Bosnian soil. The threats came thick and fast and these disturbed me deeply. Innocently and naively I had posted dates and place names for a planned visit to Bosnia on one of my web blogs. Fearing threats could become reality, I hurriedly removed the posts and refrained from advertising any further details of my visit.

I had the name, Maksim Ćulumović and I knew he was born 17th November 1909 in Brdjani / Brđani in the Province of Jajce. His parents were Jovo and Petra and I knew he'd been an Orthodox Serbian.

With very little choice, I now faced a stark reality. It was obvious, despite my painstaking efforts, which this would be as far as my search would take me for the moment. If I was to proceed any further then I would have to wait until my visit to Bosnia where I could stand on the soil that had borne my grandfather and discover the secrets it held for myself.

People often asked me why I searched for something that was long gone and could never truly be recovered. My answer was I simply desired so strongly to walk in Granddad's footsteps, to see the surroundings he had enjoyed around him, and feel the very essence of his natural environment, just as he'd done in my territorial Featherstone.

Looking back, I now know this desire was only the tip of what I searched for so passionately. At times, I would almost be pushed by something unseen, only felt, to seek out much more than a simple patch of soil that had been trodden over so many years previously.

\* \* \* \*

# Displaced

## Our Lives So Differently Told

# Chapter Seven – In the Corner of Some Foreign Field

**I swore for many years I** would never again take to the skies and fly. For over twenty years I was an avid believer in the saying that if god had wanted us to take to the skies then he would have created us bearing wings and not legs.

Now I was faced with the stark reality that unless I disputed my own fears of leaving solid ground, it was highly unlikely I would ever find whatever it was I was searching for.

I discussed the possibility of visiting Bosnia with my parents and recall Mam's attempts at dissuading me from travel. The memories of her ordeal were obvious in her words and the treatment she received in Yugoslavia, twenty years prior, was blatantly still deeply engrained and had become even more so with the atrocities which had taken place in the civil war of the 1990's.

Whatever her reasons, it was clear I should not expect any support or encouragement from her whilst I was planning any trip to Bosnia.

Bosnia; the name immediately conjures the images we have been exposed to by the media machine, eager to sell its story to the ever eager West.

Once again, I felt like the intrepid explorer who had set out so long ago now to help his Granddad who had become hopelessly lodged in a well. This time, however, my adventure was one of reality and not just borne from the cloudy imagination of a child. Never straying far from home, but with my thoughts on a distant horizon, I began preparing for a visit to Bosnia. I pondered for weeks over the alien world of foreign travel and online booking, making little progress in what would become the next step in my search.

Strangely, and for reasons unknown, Mam suddenly announced that the trip had been organised and my parents were to travel with me, despite earlier reservations and flat out refusals of help.

The three of us would fly to Split on the Croatian coast. We would spend seven days in an apartment in the resort of Makarska. During the week-long stay, we would hire a car and travel into Bosnia, to seek out, once again, Granddad's elusive birthplace. Hopefully then the search would be over, our questions would finally be answered and the unknown would be known at last.

We were to fly on September 1st 2007 which left only weeks to finalise and scrutinise the information I had.

I was convinced by now that Brdjani / Brđani on which I focused was the correct place for my search and subsequently planned routes to explore from Makarska.

The contact from Zagreb, Croatia, I had met online and who had helped me so much in my search (and also who would eventually piece together the last elements of the puzzle), translated into Bosnian the questions I planned to ask people when I reached the area. I scanned and copied the photographs of Maksim that I hoped to show people along the way and perhaps even show to those I had been searching for all along.

The day came quickly and the journey holding so many expectations for me was underway. At 2 a.m. I left home and climbed aboard the waiting car of my parents.

The streets that made up my childhood were eerily silent as the car slowly made its way through the decaying remnants of a once-proud town. Featherstone, in the darkness of the small hours, now looked lost in a bygone age which had deserted it two decades ago. Its once thriving centre, formerly home to bustling shops, revelling in united prosperity, now lay empty. Windows, once exhibiting commercial products were now boarded with warped timbers, adding to the scene of misery and decline. The whole town seemed lost in its abandonment.

Old King Coal had lost his throne and with it, the protection for his people. Generations had strived to keep the predominately socialist ideals of the working classes impassioned, many giving their lives to sustain the dream. Yet all was lost now and my eyes scanned nothing of significance besides the lingering memory of what was.

As the car reached the motorway, nerves finally crashed into me like a tsunami. It was as if I was living a dream and at any time I would be roused to join reality. Despite the extensive and never-ending research, I never once imagined I would ever walk the same path as Maksim had walked all those years before. Finally, I was to see what his own eyes had seen, to smell the same aromas and experience the hospitality of people he had missed dearly throughout his displacement.

The dream stepped up in pace and before I knew what was happening, I had boarded a Thomas Cook™ flight to Croatia.

Thankfully, the flight from Manchester airport to Split was uneventful and we touched down safely. The final fifteen minutes of the flight will perhaps stay with me forever. The sheer beauty of the Adriatic coastline was truly breathtaking and I remained transfixed to the airplane's window until our final approach. The whole coastline was interspersed with a thread of islands sitting within a few miles of the mainland. Crystal clear water added to the serenity of the scene and, once again, sadness welled within me. The beauty before my eyes had been lost forever within Granddad. The clear waters of the Adriatic had been, for him, replaced by the mud and slurry of the colliery and the vast mountain ranges had been replaced with the stinking spoil heaps of industrial Yorkshire.

Outside the airport we were directed to a minibus and within ten minutes were being driven along the winding coastal road towards Makarska. Being early September, the heat for was still unbearable for me and I was forced to take off the aged and tattered denim jacket I was renowned for wearing.

Gazing through the windows of the minibus, I was drawn to plots of land that seemed to fill every available space between the road and scattered houses. Their uniformity and neatness mirrored those of the allotment I grew up playing in and it seemed even their layout was similar in its form. The very essence of Granddad now seemed to be right here in front of me.

As I looked on in wonder it hit me that I was finally here. The place ingrained forever in my heart was finally within my gaze. I struggled throughout the journey to control my inner emotions and fought desperately to fight back the tears and failed miserably.

Tears, suppressed for so many years were now finally breaching the surface. To avoid drawing attention to my current situation and the inevitable embarrassment that would bring, I turned onto my side and feigned sleep for the rest of the journey south.

Makarska surprised me. It was not the place I had imagined. New buildings were being erected in all directions, spreading from the ancient heart of the old town. Old and new collided together, as if in competition to stake their claim on the same piece of ground.

Crowded seafront bars and cafés were interspersed with old women dressed in dark shawls and headscarves selling homemade tomatoes and cheese.

Teenagers, darting along the roads on scooters, shared the lanes with the older generation transporting farmed produce on strange, miniature, three-wheeled tractors. Old and new, merging together into one cohesive existence.

I had expected Makarska to be idyllic and slow-paced. Instead, I was met with a modern holiday resort with bustling boutiques and restaurants. New-build apartments engulfed the old quarters and spread as far as the eye could see in both directions, following the path of its shingle beaches.

Despite its apparent modern feel, it was overshadowed by the impressive backdrop of the Buckova mountains; formidable mounds that formed an impenetrable wall, seemingly pushing the town into the sea. This solid wall of stone was even more magnificent at dusk and eerily glowed golden brown as the sun slipped along its quiet path into the still Adriatic Sea.

The next couple of days were uneventful. I merely became a common tourist in this foreign land and slipped into the routine of walking along the sea front, passing by the boutiques and visiting the market in the old town. Mid afternoon I would meet with my parents and share a meal and drink with them before returning to the apartment.

My own naivety again raised its head within me. Browsing the brightly coloured football shirts on display at one of the shore front stalls I innocently asked the owner if he had any Serbian shirts.

Time it seemed stood still as everyone within close proximity stopped whatever they were doing, turning to seek out the idiot who was now within their midst.

"Be very careful my friend," the shopkeeper whispered as he leant over the wooden counter,

"Serbia is not a word we take kindly to."

Thankfully he had seen the innocence within my question and shook my hand in reassurance. He had also perhaps sensed that I was gullible and waved his farewell as I left carrying six football shirts I had just purchased more out of apology for my stupidity than need.

Evenings would be spent on the balcony taking in the beautiful views of the coastline. I always thought the east coast of England to be the most scenic and picturesque sight the eye could capture. The rolling Downs and moorland gracefully giving way to the constant advance of the waves, ordered forward with the relentless charge of the North Sea. Hidden hamlets and tiny fishing villages, as old as Father Time himself, waiting to be explored by the adventurous. How wrong I had been, I thought, as I now gazed over the silk-like smoothness of the Adriatic, now firmly seated first in my affections.

The clear seawater seemed unreal as it quietly lapped at the feet of the offshore islands. An eerie stillness hung in the air, only to be interrupted by intermittent conversation from the balconies around me. These discourses even exaggerated the dreaminess of my vision, spoken in a tongue I hardly recognised.

I had been very wrong indeed. Before me lay true beauty itself; a beauty that could never be justified by words alone. This was the place for painters and writers, a tiny snapshot offered to reveal how truly wonderful the world in which we live is. A place of peace and tranquillity very few of us could ever imagine unless we had seen it with our own eyes.

The following days passed far too quickly, as they do for most of us away from the daily rigours of the workplace. Visits to the local market and hours spent strolling along the seafront were now replaced with planning for the next and final part of my adventure. Carefully, I mapped out the winding route that would take us north and onwards into a country only seen by most from the comfort of their armchairs whilst taking in the horrors of war often broadcast on news bulletins.

7 a.m. on the Wednesday we left Makarska in the hire car that we had collected the previous evening. Prior to leaving,

Dad and I engaged in a debate over currency. He was adamant when we entered Bosnia the Euro would be honoured; I was not so convinced and said we should exchange money into Bosnian Markas before we left Croatia. In a fatherly way, he ridiculed my suggestion.

"After all," he cajoled, "you are hardly a world wide traveller!"

Looking back, I was foolish to succumb to his belief that through his personal experience he knew everything I did not about world travel. But I did succumb, so we left Makarska with only Croatian Kunas and the all-important Euro.

\* \* \* \*

# Displaced

## Our Lives So Differently Told

## Chapter Eight – Walking in the Footsteps

**We drove along the coastline heading north** and rising rapidly over the mountain range that had dominated the skyline in Makarska. Before long, the ground levelled and I was amazed at the sheer beauty before my eyes. For miles the countryside was a series of rolling hills, met with mountain ranges distant on all sides. Finally, this was the place I had pictured in my mind. The place that had been lost to Granddad so many years ago, confined to the very depths of his memory, lay here before me as if it was his very essence staring back through the mist of time.

Within thirty minutes of our departure we were stopped at a border crossing. The four uniformed men reminded me more of Hollywood extras then they did officers of the law.

Thankfully, and very briefly, I found myself transported to a disturbing movie scene I had watched as a teenager. *Midnight Express* portrayed the horrors of a Turkish prison and the men now approaching our parked car resembled the guards in the film. Slightly unkempt despite the formal uniform and with the air of danger about them, they walked in a slow circle around us. Maybe they had seen few tourists before and could not understand why we were leaving behind the beauty of the Adriatic coastline for what lay beyond. It was obvious they were curious about our arrival. Time seemed to stand still as our paperwork was checked and processed. Whatever it had been that had aroused interest quickly diminished and we were waved through to continue our journey.

As we drove through, it hit me; I was in Bosnia at last. This was the place I had searched for so long and as we travelled further I could feel Granddad's presence rising within me, the driving force that had taken me this far surfacing as it's own entity in this strange land.

Everything I now saw reminded me of the great man I knew. For the first time I was sure I was on the right path, travelling forwards at speed now, ready to know the truth.

Driving north, it soon became obvious the terrible hardships the country had suffered in the 1990's. Grave markers littered the landscape in hurriedly put together cemeteries occupying every available scrap of land.

Small hamlets now devoid of human life, their decaying buildings displaying the vivid scars of madness and war. Scorched walls left pock marked from artillery and small arms fire. The despair and cruelty that had taken place within the confines of the now sad and broken buildings jumping out from every shadow. The horror and disbelief which must have been felt when the inhabitants realised the rest of the world had simply turned their backs on them hit me as I surveyed the land before me.

Once thriving villages where children had played and the aged residents had congregated to idly gossip were now forever silent. It seemed even the ghosts had long since fled the horror, the mass grave, looking elsewhere for their final salvation. It would not be found here.

Even the occasional buildings that remained occupied displayed their own battle scars with their exteriors riddled with the wounds of gunfire. I struggled in vain to fight back my emotions. A deep sense of loss and suffering for a people I had never known. Embarrassed, I constantly feigned tiredness, yawning to cover watery eyes whilst making attempts at small talk. It was obvious the same feelings of despair were washing over Mam as we slowly drove through this graveyard. Tears readily spread across her cheeks as she gave in to her emotions, no longer even attempting to be brave.

Beauty and the beast came to mind as we travelled on. The beauty of the countryside stood in stark contrast to the reared head of the beast, man's ability to cause suffering to his own kin evident on the darkened earth and decimated dwellings interrupting the beautiful scenery as a sobering reminder.

The journey through central Bosnia passed slowly, but without incident. I amazed myself with my navigation skills in a foreign country with road signs that were unreadable. It was well known amongst my colleagues that if anyone needed to get lost on a straight road then I was the man for the job. On more than one occasion I had to telephone the office and describe my surroundings just to make it to training events, yet here, I managed with little failure.

However, just as I thought things were going well and I would be recorded in the annals of history as one of the great explorers, we encountered our first stumbling block.

Strangely the manageable road signs switched from the Latin alphabet to that of the Cyrillic one. The same alien letters I had encountered over twenty years previously during the miner's strike of 1984.

Russian miners had taken pity on our desperate plight and shipped food containers to help ward off malnutrition amongst the mining communities. One particular tinned 'goodie' soon became my favourite and I would consume as much of this sandwich paste as possible. Unfortunately, as the months passed, supplies of my favourite spread became hard to come by. Remembering how Granddad had once revealed he could speak Russian, I presented him with the last tin, in the hope I could purchase something similar in England.

"Baby food." Came his reply as he idly scanned the outer wrapping.

"From six months upwards." He added with a smile.

Baby food! No wonder my waistline had been growing in girth despite the hardships we endured. I had been innocently feasting on pure protein and fat...

Now the master navigator and map-reader was helpless. I had simply not taken into account the use of different alphabets. Looking back I had been foolish and naïve to have overlooked this. Aunty Mary, Mam's elder sister, had years earlier taken a summer holiday to the former Yugoslavia. She became friendly with a local bar owner and asked him to write a simple hello message for Granddad. On her return home I recall clearly as if yesterday, she excitedly passed Granddad the slip of paper. With a look of distaste he simply screwed up the paper and tossed it into the glowing embers of the kitchen coal fire.

"Wrong alphabet." He said simply. Years later I suspected whatever had been written had not been the words of warmth and greeting. Given the deep cultural and religious divides within Yugoslavia I suspected the simple message might have been no more than 'hate mail', venomous words aimed at the unknown recipient. Now I suspect different. Maybe Granddad was indeed only fluent with the written Cyrillic alphabet.

Writing this now I know what I did not then, the illegible road signs were the invisible crossing border which separated the Croatian / Muslim Federation from the Serbian dominated Republika Srspska.

To make matters worse, this was when the weather began to close in. Storm clouds descended as if conjured up by magic and within thirty minutes daylight was replaced with darkness as we became caught in a fierce thunderstorm the likes of which I have never experienced before.

The torrential cascade of rainwater now made progress slow on the mountain roads and it was not long before I feared we were becoming hopelessly lost.

We had driven north from the Croatian coast, into the beautiful wilderness that is Bosnia without interruption, yet for some reason we foreigners were suddenly being noticed. Waves and shouts greeted us as we passed through remote villages. Naivety once again reared its head and we innocently waved back returning what we thought was greeting and yet now I recognise as scorn.

I was the foolish Brit that entered Serbian territory in a hired vehicle bearing Croatian registration plates. Maybe it is just the use of scare tactics, maybe it is harsh words of warning, but I know now I had placed not only myself, but also my parents in danger.

It turned out my naivety would accompany me throughout my search.

Daylight still diminished in the raging storm, we happened to drive past an isolated farmhouse just as an elderly couple were stepping outside the rough wooden door.

Eagerly, and desperately, we pulled the car to a stop. I jumped out and walked towards them, offering greetings with the customary "dobra jutro" (good afternoon) just to sound impressive. Impress them I must have as their reply was in high speed Bosnian, the translation of which I had no idea.

I was intrigued by the elderly couple as we exchanged words none of us could understand. They were picture postcard images of what you would expect from rural Bosnia. Their clothes and even their shoes were primitive and hand fashioned. The heavy woollen trousers they wore were obviously woven from wool gathered from their own sheep running free on the mountain slopes and the leather, sandal like footwear was the obvious result of using all of the animal by-product.

I showed the elderly man the writing I had prepared and his eyes caught my own. In that instant, I felt myself looking into the eyes of Maksim.

They say the eyes are the windows to the soul and that they betray the true life a man has led. One moment they could be the large, proud eyes of a man who could rise above anything just by using the power of his mind. The next they could became sharp and narrow like those of a wild, untamed animal, surviving on instinct alone. Then there could be the laughing eyes of a kind, warm hearted, generous man, carefree, maybe even happy.

Twelve months later I would learn that the surviving brother Maksim had left in Bosnia had the same ability to engage and transfix you with his eyes, whilst slowly but surely scrutinising every aspect of you open to him.

With finger pointing the elderly man traced the words written on the piece of paper. He repeated the word 'Šipovo' and smiled as he pointed down the road in the direction that we were travelling. The woman, smiling, opened the rough wooden door which was the entrance to their humble home and gestured me inside.

Without wanting to appear rude, I stepped inside behind her and her husband and was immediately handed a tiny shot glass of Slivovitz. The liquid burnt my throat and I could see the amusement on the couple's faces as I fought back the cough. The woman eagerly offered more of the fiery brandy but I offered my excuses the best I could. Here I was faced with human good will and kindness, which is in short supply in the modern world. It was obvious this elderly couple had little in the way of wealth nor of creature comforts. I shuddered to imagine the horrors they had endured throughout the civil war. Despite their hardship, however, they welcomed their unknown guest with open arms and warmth, the likes of which I had never experienced within my own native homeland.

I thanked them for their hospitality and headed back to the waiting car. With one final look back and a wave of farewell we headed onwards, along the tree-lined road, glistening in the pouring rain.

Maybe it was the shot of Slivovitz racing through my bloodstream like some hallucinogenic drug, but I felt closer to the nature all around me after my encounter. Maybe the scenery was simply engulfing me in its sheer beauty. Pine forests on both sides of the beaten road gave way to rugged outcrops of rock and we found ourselves dropping gently down whilst small cliffs rose above us in steep, impenetrable walls of stone. It gave the illusion that at some point in time, a great engineer had striven to forge the road from deep in the mountainside, cutting through all in his path. Maybe the real reason was simply modern man had followed an ancient trail through this magnificent landscape, laying down the foundations of a road in its footsteps.

I closed my eyes and imagined what it must have been like for Maksim to slowly over time, lose the beauty of his country of origin. To wake each and every day in the hope of catching one last glimpse and instead having it replaced by the industrial decay of King Coal Yorkshire.

Even the oppressive weather added to the beauty being set out before my eyes, not to the misery as it did at home.

Now, only the occasional gutted ruin of once quaint little family homes gave away the pain of the 90's. The rain seemed to drown out all other sounds as each heavy droplets crashed noisily onto the car roof, only to be amplified within its interior.

The road was deserted of other vehicles but occasionally we would pass lone figures walking by its side. Like the old couple before, they were dressed in simple clothes, and appeared as if they were lost in time, taking a stroll to nowhere in the pouring rain and in no great hurry to get to their destination.

Eventually the road levelled and, turning sharply to the left, I saw Pliva River for the first time. Like the land around me, the sight of this stretch of water was breathtaking. For months prior I had searched for this place and now here it lay before me.

Granddad always spoke of Pliva and swimming. Now, looking at the green, slow flowing waters, I was shaken by the stark realisation that I was finally here, so close to the reality of a place that I had dreamt of for decades.

In those very waters, I felt I could almost touch the soul and spirit of the man I lost. My need to seek the truth was stronger than ever.

The road cut through the landscape as it wound upstream with the green flow of Pliva to our right. Although the already dismal weather worsened still, my spirits were at fever pitch and I knew that the town of Šipovo lay within a few miles. More importantly, the hamlet of Brdjani / Brđani was within a twenty minute drive from the town.

Occasionally now we would be met with oncoming traffic, a clear indicator we were finally approaching a populated area. At first it shocked me at how badly the Bosnians drove. More and more of the oncoming traffic seemed to wander across the road into our path, forcing our car to swerve erratically to avoid a collision. Then I began to remember the old couple's hospitality and the fiery brandy they had offered so early in the day and assumed maybe people here drank without giving thought to the consequences before taking to the road. As the instances of being forced off the road increased the dreadful truth finally dawned on me. We had hired the car in

Croatia. I remember looking it over before our journey and pondering over the red chequered flag on the registration plate. The flag of Croatia was greeting oncoming travellers and with the hatred still felt between the two sides, it became obvious that the straying of the oncoming vehicles was not accidental, but rather a desire to see us in a burnt out heap at the roadside!

Not wishing to worry my already anguished parents any further, I kept my realisation to myself and hid the true extent of the danger we could now be in.

We travelled on, running parallel to Pliva on a winding course that mirrored the rivers bends and straights and entered the town of Šipovo. The heavy rain continued and the only people visible were a group of teenagers who jeered as we drove past.

Mam seemed surprised at the youngster's interest in our arrival and I played the situation down by claiming it was evident we were newcomers to this close-knit community and therefore a sight rarely seen.

Regardless, here I was at last in a place I had been exploring online for months prior to my arrival. Satellite images had given me a real sense of the place and I remembered the towns layout from memory.

At least I thought I did. As we encountered the first road junction, it became evident that none of the signs were eligible in the native Cyrillic lettering and we drove through the town with heavy hearts and the air of disappointment filling the cars interior.

We pulled into the first petrol station we came across. The fuel gauge registered less than half a tank of petrol and besides, this would be a good place to seek out directions. Even before the car had fully come to a stand-still the attendant dashed across from the confines of the small shop and stood, in the pouring rain, banging on the drivers side window. Maybe he just wanted a fast sale in the torrential weather, or maybe, like the oncoming traffic, he had been infuriated with the red flag embellished on the cars registration plate.

Whatever the reason I quickly got out of the car and stood facing him in the drenching rain. His anger was evident in the fast flowing, words he spat at me.

My own, innocent reply was simply,

"Hello, how are you?"

With these simple words his arms lowered and the grimace which engulfed his face slowly subsided into a smile. The upraised arms encircled my shoulders and he held me tightly, almost squeezing the air from my lungs as he laughed.

My own laugh came forth and we stood, in the rain, holding each other and laughing like two crazy men, realising for the first time the punch line to a joke long since told.

With renewed confidence that I was not to be the victim of a vicious roadside assault, I offered my new-found friend the paper with the translated questions. Like the elderly man before, he carefully scrutinised the writing, tracing it with his finger.

It was obvious there was something on the paper which interested him as he pointed to some of the words. In the direction we had travelled from whilst speaking quickly. I looked and could only shrug my shoulders as he repeated the words "Chulum, Chulum." Although both parties were equally enthusiastic to get their message across, it soon became evident we were both were fighting a losing battle and we shrugged our shoulders in unison. Despite my preparation and planning, the language barrier had simply beaten me.

Remembering that we were running low on fuel I pointed to the cars fuel cap and held out both Croatian Kuna and Euros. The shrugged shoulders and outstretched arms appeared again and I could understand the words "No Kuna, no Euro, only Marka." It was obvious the only currency that would be accepted here was the Bosnian Marka, the one currency I was travelling without.

With a strong grip of the hand and heavy pat on the back we said our farewells and I clambered, down hearted, back into the car. The realisation slowly sank in. I was so close to what I desired, but still so far as we headed back in the direction we had travelled.

The whole journey had simply been wasted. The one chance I had of finally reaching my goal and, possibly unveiling the secrets it held, had slipped from my weary grasp, just as I thought I was to hold it in my hands at least.

Begrudgingly, we left Šipovo. The dark oppressive gloom of its weather only exaggerated my own bitter feelings of disappointment.

Although the road signs offered no hint of our direction, I knew that if we followed the path of the winding River Pliva, it would take us further north to the town of Jajce. Although this course would be taking us further from the Croatian border, it would lead us into the Federation of Bosnia. Road signs would be in the Latin alphabet and I could plot a course back into Makarska.

Within thirty minutes we had entered the deserted streets of Jajce and could make out its castle in the skyline, blurred by dense cloud and rainfall, but still imposing regardless of natures best efforts.

The famous waterfall eluded us and we drove on. Sheer slopes of densely packed pine trees reared up on both sides and rather than make the scenery look ominous, the dark clouds and rain only seemed to magnify its natural beauty and mystery.

The rest of the journey went smoothly and without running out of fuel we returned to the same border crossing we had encountered at the beginning. The same officers checked our papers and solemnly waved us through, back into Croatia. Before long we were parking the car at the hotel and making our way to the apartment.

The next two days were spent simply enjoying the sun and wandering around the seafront and market, more to pass the time than for enjoyment or relaxation. In truth, I yearned to return home as quickly as possible. My heart was heavy with disappointment and being so close to everything I sought only seemed to exaggerate the feeling.

Thankfully, the days passed quickly and we landed at Manchester airport without delay.

As I sat in a different car in a different country, heading to a home hundreds of miles away from where I had left a part of my hope, and myself I had to wonder whether I was wasting my time, whether Maksim even had a past or if it had been erased forever.

I felt like the monster or UFO hunter, never actually getting to experience a sighting of their own, but relying more on other people's accounts to pin their hopes and dreams on.

Down hearted, I began to wonder if everyone had been right from the very beginning and I would never find the answers I so desperately craved no matter how hard I tried.

\* \* \* \*

# Displaced
## Our Lives So Differently Told

## Chapter Nine - Down this road we've been so many times

**Over the following weeks, I gathered my** thoughts together and mapped out exactly what I had achieved in all the time I had been searching. In stark truth, I had little more than what my Grandfather himself had given away, talking to me as a boy.

I had documents relating to his time in Displaced Persons camps in Italy, Germany and the UK that outlined his basic information. I had photographs taken before the war and one item of correspondence from a sister-in-law who, in the immediate years following World War II, had been living in Montenegro.

The realisation slowly dawned on me, I had achieved nothing. Certainly nothing of consequence.

The blog pages I created in the hope of having just one hit had not born a single fruit. Despite over twenty thousands visitors, most of which had followed links from Yugoslavian Genealogy forums, there was no recognition, no missing piece of the jigsaw puzzle.

Private Genealogy Investigators based in the former Yugoslavia found no connection either, despite numerous telephone calls to families with the same surname in Croatia,

Bosnia and Serbia. Military historians in Serbia had been contacted, but they too could find no trace of Ćulumović in the 2$^{nd}$ Korpus Ravna Gore that Maksim had been photographed with in 1941, near the town of Čacak in Serbia.

Despite the complete lack of progress I found myself drawn to the search, as if being pushed along and directed by unseen hands. It felt almost like a magnetic pull, urging me to dig deeper and deeper, to remove the shroud and uncover what was really there and had been there all along.

I would refer back to the photographs I had in my possession. Firstly, images from the 1950's, where he would pose, tall and proud and secondly, photographs of an ailing man, shying away from the lens in the years before his death 30 years later.

I recall in my adolescent years it was forbidden to take any photographs of Granddad. He would shy away instantly if any camera came into view, yet his response to my crude toy rifle would even eclipse even this reaction as I once found out to my detriment. Like all young children, lost in the excitement a new toy brings, I remember running the short distance from my own home to his to show off my new acquisition. The fearless freedom fighter charged into the living room and took careful aim at his target, bespectacled, scanning the day's horse racing reports in the morning newspaper. However, before the finger trigger had any chance to fire off an imaginary projectile, the gun lay shattered, beyond repair, across the carpet. Despite the advances of old age, it was obvious the man's reactions remained as quick as those of a coiled spring. Whatever he had experienced in his life prior rose to the fore as he acted swiftly and without conscious thought to protect himself. He had simply seen and acted. In that one second I was transformed from the child with the plastic 3.03 rifle to the taker of life he knew only too well. I remember the tear in his eye as he realised what he had done, holding me tight to his chest in soothing comfort.

It became apparent whilst I researched that almost no photographs existed of the man between his initial arrival in the UK and his death there in the 1980's. I recall how he would often change his appearance, constantly shaving his head and growing a moustache, at times a full beard. I would ask him why and he would simply imply this was for religious purposes, an answer he knew would be accepted as a satisfactory response and settle any curiosity.

My research led me to believe that simply, he was afraid and working hard to hide his true identity. Post war Yugoslavia under Josip Broz had built a highly efficient Secret Police known as the UDBA. Anyone considered by the organisation to be enemies of the country would be targeted and assassinated. Individuals that had fled Yugoslavia could be, depending on their reasons for exile, considered enemies of the socialist regime. There are records of international assassinations including such killings in the UK.

Maybe this was the reason for the secrecy Maksim enveloped himself in. Maybe too this was also the reason He had always slept with a steel bar beneath the bed. Not the fear of impending burglary, but the deep rooted fear of being found, targeted and cruelly dispatched as so many others of his kind had been throughout the world.

Although he would never speak about anything to do with the war it was obvious he was a highly respected figure within the Serbian community.

My parents recall whenever he entered a room everyone would rise without hesitation. In group conversation, everyone would speak English if he were there. As soon as he left, the conversation would switch to their native Serbian tongue and English would only be spoken again when he reappeared. Mam told me she always suspected the reason for this strange ritual was that whilst he was not present he had no control over what was said and would not want the wrong thing to be mentioned and give even a hint to the secrets he carried.

The following months were spent feeling downhearted and beaten. I started the search with little, if any hope of ever finding out any information, but as I progressed, my hopes had been constantly raised and then sent crashing down again as if on a never ending rollercoaster. I had, however, always bounced back with determination and resilience. Simply picking up the pieces of the puzzle only to start again. This time though, I felt well and truly beaten and made it obvious to those around me. I sent to an email to an online friend in Zagreb who had helped me so much wherever he could and he replied despite every set back, every dead end I had encountered he had never felt such a feeling of defeat than that in the letter I had sent him. He urged me to continue and this was just another stumbling block which should not halt me in what I was attempting to do.

His reply renewed me. Deep down I knew I had to take my search to the end of its course regardless. He urged me to go back to the very beginning and that is exactly what I did.

I started with the photograph that had been sent from Bijelo Polje in Montenegro which had been signed by a sister-in-law. A sister in-law who looked almost identical to the woman in another photograph that was signed by his wife.

The friend in Zagreb kindly contacted the local radio station in Bijelo Polje to see if they could either shed some light on the story or identify the people in the photograph. Despite the photographs and correspondence being circulated, still no one came forward either to offer information or to acknowledge any recognition of the people in the photographs. At this point, yet another lead in my search came to a dead end. The only lead connecting real people to a real place was left still without meaning or understanding.

Throughout these months I had constantly checked and double-checked the paperwork and photographs I had. It was always the people's faces that would draw my gaze as I would look into their eyes in an attempt to decipher any secrets hidden there, but found none, only long forgotten memories.

It was as if the photographs drew me back to a time in Granddads life before I even existed. Each time I would curse and regret deeply I had never pushed him a little more when he had announced he was to write a book. The memories would have been etched in those pages, the mystery would have been solved and I would not be left wondering, lost.

I turned full circle once again in my search and looked at the other villages in both Bosnia and Serbia with the name Brđani. I mailed tourist boards from the areas covering the villages, but got no reply.

Hours each day I was once again spending scanning the Internet for any clues or avenues I had not tried.

Then came the ultimate breakthrough that within months would not only lead me to the truth, but would also see me walking the footsteps I longed for in Bosnia.

I had corresponded online with a photographer who had posted his work on the Pliva region. He had lived in the town of Šipovo prior to the civil war and although he had no recollection of any Ćulumović families from the area, he did know of a Ćulum who had lived in the village of Brđani.

He also remembered that Ostoja Ćulum had been a well-known and respected figure in the community.

Unfortunately however, Ostoja had died twenty years previously in 1987.

He fondly recalled that children would shout "Chulum" and hide whenever Ostoja walked past and how he would hold captive an audience with his amusing stories.

The name 'Chulum' jolted me and my mind raced back to the meeting I had with Bogdan, the surviving refugee still living in England. I remember passing him a photograph of Granddad and how he immediately exclaimed the word "Chulum!" I recall even more how the man's wife had almost spat the words "That was not his name!" as if he had broadcast a profound obscenity.

I was later to find out Granddad had been a very good friend of Bogdan's wife Boja's father, and they had known each other before the outbreak of war. It was obvious, looking back, that the secret code of silence had been innocently breached, but immediately sealed tight once again.

I immediately passed this information to the friend in Zagreb and the private investigators in Montenegro.

My friend, ever efficient, replied the next day with renewed hope and enthusiasm. It was again obvious he had given up his own precious free time to help me in my once more desperate search.

He passed onto me e-mail addresses he had found online of Ćulum families living in and around the Mirkonjic Grad area, a town north of Šipovo. As he suggested, I emailed each of the names listed, about twenty in total, explaining briefly my search for family information and asking if they had any connection or knowledge of Ćulum families having lived in the village of Brđani.

Agonising weeks slowly crept by as I constantly checked and rechecked my e-mail inbox. Once again my hopes were fading fast and it seemed another lead was slipping from me. When I had all but given up, I finally received a response. It was from an Ćulum family and although not directly related to my search, they did verify there had been families with the same name living in Brđani and, that in a fit of generosity, they would visit the village themselves to try and find out more.

From then, the weeks trudged slowly on with nothing but this email to offer me. Again, I had reached the dizzy heights of the rollercoaster, only to be hurtled earthwards in disappointment..

As if my search was not already complicated enough, I now faced a new dilemma. The email correspondence, it appeared, was between myself and a child. Even taking into account the language barrier, the words were not written by an adult. Coupled with the fact that "Vanja" had used the pen name of "Jonny Depp" I became convinced the reply had come from a minor.

I felt all progress slipping away as each and every day passed. With the internet now seen as a playground for predators preying on the innocent naivety of children, I knew it would not be wise, however well intentioned, to pursue the attentions of a child online. My breakthrough slowly slipped from within my grasp and once again I became filled with the feelings of failure.

Out of sheer desperation, I again looked to the private investigators in Montenegro and they vowed to make telephone contact with all Ćulum families living in the Mirkonjic Grad area.

True to their word I received good news the following day. By chance, they had telephoned the first Ćulum family living within the town at the centre of my new found optimism. Remarkably, it was the father of Vanja who answered the telephone, confirming that his family were in the process of visiting the elusive village of Brđani to aid an Englishman in his quest to uncover the family history. He went onto explain

Vanja had discussed his earlier online contact with me and the family were all too willing to help. First, they had family business to attend to in Belgrade, and then they would visit the village and investigate on my behalf.

Fully realising the hardships and financial struggle still being felt in Bosnia, I offered to incur any expenses. Bosnian pride rose however and I regret the family may have been a little offended of my offer of financial aid. I was assured a visit the village would take place at no cost to me and they would help in any way they could.

Slowly, days became weeks and I felt abandoned once more. Maybe I had relied too much on a family I had never met nor spoken with other than to ask a great favour.

Returning from a particularly stressful day at work I turned on the computer, coffee in hand, readying myself for the countless trash and spam emails that seemed to target me. Countless millionaires over the years had offered me their inheritance in return for my banking details and so many prizes had been won without me even having bothered to enter.

One email immediately caught my attention and was headed "Jonny Depp". It was from Vanja's family.

They apologized for their lateness, but more than made up for it in the information they had discovered.

They had gone to the village and spoken with an elderly woman. Astonishingly, she remembered Maksim and relayed to the family that he had indeed lived in the village. She remembered clearly he had disappeared during the horrific years of World War II. As to his whereabouts after that, she had never known. She had never seen nor heard of him since.

The woman, whose name I was later to learn was Petra Grubac, also verified Maksim was the younger brother to Ostoja Ćulum. She very kindly walked with the family to show them not only the grave of Ostoja, but also the family home which was remarkably still standing. deign Even more remarkable, Petra could recall long lost events from the family's history, 60 years in the past. She relayed only the two brothers and a daughter had survived the brutal and murderous attack on the village in 1941. Ostoja had remarried she said, but after his death in 1987, the wife had moved to Serbia.

More importantly, Petra disclosed there were indeed living relations with whom she would make contact and pass on my information. She would let Maksim's family know that finally someone was desperately looking to make contact.

I couldn't take it in. Was Ostoja the lost brother I remember Granddad speaking of as he sat me upon his knee as a child, briefly reliving hazy days of his own childhood full of mischief and mayhem?

Was he the older brother Maksim would idle away the day with swimming and frolicking beneath waterfalls hidden in the curve of the Pliva River? Would these two men, then boys, steal away plum brandy from the elders and get hopelessly drunk, hidden away from sight within the thick blanket of surrounding woodlands?

After so many years of relentless searching and constant disappointment, finally here was a living person who could actually remember Granddad on his native soil.

Four photographs were also attached to the email. With shaking hands I selected the first and waited with baited breath as it slowly downloaded. Immediately, I was transfixed by the image opening before me. It was a house perched on a gentle slope of grass and plum trees. The structure was fashioned from wood with a stone base and steeply pointed roof. It was the kind of house that conjured up images of the children's novel Hansel and Gretel. In just this one photograph, I knew deep in my gut that I had finally found what I was so desperately searching for. Granddads very essence poured from the wooden structure before me.

I was drawn back to the wooden sheds he had built on his beloved allotment. This little house was there in each and every one of them. I now realized he had replicated everything he had known and loved into his new found surroundings. He had cocooned himself in the familiar, to feel safe and secure, but also to remember.

I knew for the first time I was looking deep into the very memories that had followed Maksim to his death. I was now seeing what he had seen before he was torn from the people and surroundings he knew.

The second photograph was of a grave. Ostoja Ćulum stared back at me from eyes fixed menacingly in the cabriole china photograph immortalised on the stone marker.

Sadness filled me with the knowledge that the two brothers never knew the path each of their lives had taken. They must have thought of each other every day for forty years, until they left this world a mere twelve months apart. I had not been the only one carrying around unanswered questions.

The last two photographs were of an elderly lady sitting in the rough wooden porch that was the entrance to her humble home. Petra Grubac, the woman who still remembered Granddad, sixty years on from his sudden departure, now looked up at me from the computer screen. I so desperately wanted to reach out and touch her, make sure she was real. Gravestones and wooden houses are objects and cannot tell their stories. This woman, however, could. She was the missing piece I needed to make sense of this 20 year old puzzle.

Not that this information would sink in. I scrutinized every word over and over again, looking for anything which could be incorrect, sure a mistake had been made. I sat for days looking at the emails and photographs, looking for something we'd all missed, but there was nothing there.

Realization slowly dawned and I had to face the fact this new information might actually be correct.

The name 'Chulum' had been the key, hiding in plain sight, right under my nose. Even in his early signatures, the clues were there. He would write Ćulum in bold and a much lighter 'ović' as if he had momentarily forgotten his name and had added the latter as an afterthought.

The next few weeks passed without further news. I found myself impatient so close now to learning the truth and putting everything to rest, yet knowing I would have to have contact with any living relatives of Maksim's in Bosnia before I reached my ultimate goal.

My entire life, I had been told that everyone had been killed during the war and no family survived there and so it had never occurred to me I would have any family to meet.

My only desire had been to trace my grandfather's birthplace and see it for myself.

But now, everything was different. Not only had they survived the carnage of WWII when the village had been destroyed and the family left devastated, but they had also lived to see history repeat itself in the brutal civil war of the 90's.

Just as I was starting to get over the initial shock, I received another email that left me stunned. I had to read the short message over and over again to comprehend the crudely spelt words as well as the information held within.

It was from Mile, Ostoja Ćulum's grandson. He verified Maksim had been his long lost Great Uncle. He knew from family stories Granddad had escaped to England immediately after the Second World War had ended. Mile said he had read my blog with interest and would very much like to speak with me, including his telephone number in his details.

Although he spoke very little English, his youngest son, Saša (pronounced Sasha) did, and he told me I should telephone when the boy was home, anytime after 6pm.

After sitting anxiously all afternoon, my natural lack of patience got the better of me and, unable to wait any longer, I dialled the telephone number with trembling hands at exactly 5.30pm. I was wracked with nerves as I heard the pulsing of the dial tone on the other end of the line. Just as my emotions were about to get the better of me and I was about to place the receiver back in its cradle, I was stopped by the sound of a woman's voice, speaking in a Bosnian tongue. Cautiously I said hello and asked for Mile. Words I could not understand were spoken back in return. Again I said the name Mile and that I was calling from England. I could hear fumbling and voices and then I heard someone say,

"Hello, how are you?" in broken English.

The male voice relayed that his name was Saša and he was Mile's son. He went on to say Mile was there with him in the room and he would translate the conversation for us.

It was immediately obvious from the speedily spoken conversation in the background, that the family were delighted Granddad had survived and now, after all these years, they would learn of his life after his escape.

Despite my initial excitement, disbelief swept over me once more. Maybe Mile, like me, was ready to grasp any straw coincidence could offer. Maksim, after all, was quite a common name and their must have been countless Maksim's who had fled to foreign lands to escape the communists. I remembered the resettlement documents I held, paperwork created when Granddad first arrived in Italy.

Name, date of birth and parents name immediately flashed from memory.

"Saša," I asked hesitantly, "Ask Mile if he knows the name of his great grandfather?"

Words I could not understand were spoken in the background before a clear voice said "Jovo."

In that instance I felt as if the whole world was about to swallow me whole. Maybe, with the story finally settling into place, I had finally gotten it right. Granddad's resettlement documentation referred to his place of birth as being Brđani and he would speak of swimming in Pliva, the river that passes by the village. More importantly, the paperwork recorded his parent's names were Jovo and Petra.

I would also learn Jovo had been killed in 1914 fighting the Turks in Sollun, now part of Greece. Granddad would have been five years old when his father had died. Already born into a world of hardship and uncertainty this explains how he would briefly recall having a poor upbringing and being breastfed well into adolescence. How his mother Petra must have struggled rearing a young family on her own.

In that very first telephone conversation, I was made so welcome and was immediately invited to travel to Bosnia where I would be their honoured guest and finally get to visit the place I had merely glimpsed, through my own experiences and the memory of my Grandfather.

We arranged another telephone conversation for the following week and I promised to check available flights to Sarajevo without further delay.

I then received another email. The simple headline read – "Petra's Daughter."

I remember the strange feeling of apprehension as I clicked to open the message. I took a deep breath and read. It was from Vesna, Mile's sister. Her Mam had been Petra, the daughter to Ostoja Ćulum. Vesna had spoken to Mile about me and had also visited the blog pages I had online.

She explained that she had suffered a similar fate to Maksim and had fled Bosnia to live in the USA after the civil war. It saddened me to think yet again, the same family, albeit different generations, had been displaced through warfare. History certainly does like to repeat itself.

I waited until morning to call Vesna. I was unsure of the time difference between the UK and the USA, but for some reason I assumed the time zone in the States was in front of our own.

The first call was at 9am but there was no reply and I left a brief message on the answer phone. When I arrived at work I was dismayed to discover from a colleague that America is behind our time and I had in fact called in the early hours of the morning.

Later that day, I received a voice-mail on my mobile phone. It was Vesna asking me to telephone her.

With trembling hands I carefully dialed the number and waited with baited breath as I once again listened to a pulsating dial tone. After what seemed like an eternity I heard a woman's voice say hello. I introduced myself and the excitement was evident in both our voices as we exchanged pleasantries.

Vesna explained she had been told of Maksim by her Mam and had known he had indeed survived the war and went on to live in England.

Her Mam spoke of him and said that she could remember letters arriving from England early after the war, but these letters had been destroyed by the authorities before they could be read.

I would learn months later that it had been a single act of human stupidity which had torn the family apart for good.

Soon after the end of World War II, Ostoja had been repairing a boundary fence separating his property from that of a neighbour. Being a crude and cumbersome workman to say the least, the repair may not have been to master craftsman standard. Unfortunately, the neighbour discovered that one his bulls had died after becoming impaled on one of the poorly constructed timbers protruding from the wooden barrier. A fierce argument ensued, leaving both parties bitter enemies.

Months later Ostoja bumped into the local post master from the nearby town of Šipovo. Excitedly the postmaster innocently asked if the letter was indeed from Maksim. He went onto explain he had been on his way to visit Ostoja with a letter that had arrived from England when he had came across the aggrieved neighbour. Knowing nothing of the ongoing dispute, he had innocently given the letter to the neighbour, who offered to save him the journey. Ostoja never received the letter.

I suspect the letter was not simply disposed of. Earlier in my search I was told Granddad had received a visit from the local police with a letter, allegedly from family. The contents of the letter remain a mystery to this day. Whatever had been penned on those pages however enraged him and the paper was immediately destroyed in the glowing embers of the kitchens coal fire.

In that one act of selfish and childish revenge, the neighbour ensured Granddad would go to his grave forty years later, never knowing his brother had survived the carnage of war.

Vesna expanded and explained her Mam, Petra had also known that Maksim had survived the war and displacement, ending up somewhere in England, but even the name Petra raised the hairs on my neck. The name, for whatever reason had been instilled in my childhood memory. If I ever envisaged a Yugoslavian woman in my minds eye, she was always called Petra. Why I do not know, as Granddad had never once used this name in his faltered recollections of his early life.

Petra had also been the mother of Maksim. The mother he had fondly recalled as being in constant hiding from him as he searched out her breast milk up until the age of seven years old. Petra had been the name Maksim's brother, Ostoja, had passed down to his own daughter, the daughter whose own children would now provide me with all the answers I had been searching for.

As the following days slowly unfolded, my initial excitement turned to a deep feeling of dread. I had searched only for the soil, not a family I never knew survived. I had looked for a ghost and instead had found flesh and blood. I was in new territory greatly removed from my wildest hopes and dreams and I had to now concentrate on Vesna, who seemed as convinced as I was that I should travel to Bosnia and finally come face to face with Brđani and within it, Maksim's past.

Mile readily agreed with his sister and invited me to visit him in his hometown of Novi Travnik. He offered to collect me at the airport in Sarajevo, have me as a guest in his apartment and drive me to the birthplace of my Granddad. I happily agreed.

However, the word 'Sarajevo' filled me with apprehension. The name only conjured up images of death and mindless destruction; it had been the epicentre of the Bosnian war. As the capital city, all sides were desperate for their flag to fly there. During the 1990's, it had become nothing more than a killing field. I recalled only too vividly the news footage of death in the streets, innocent civilians murdered by mortar and sniper fire as they had desperately foraged for food and water, scarce in wartime conditions.

Sniper Alley was a name that became infamous throughout the world. Heavily besieged, this area of Sarajevo had become a hunting ground for the deadly snipers. Men, women and children alike were seen as legitimate targets in a war which held no rules. Here, there was no Geneva Convention or codes of modern warfare. Sarajevo, like the rest of Bosnia, had turned its back on humanity and compassion. Records now indicate, during the city's siege, snipers wounded over one thousand and thirty civilians, killing two hundred and twenty five. In a sick twist, sixty of those had been children.

Despite my fear of Sarajevo, I knew, deep down I would have to overcome this if I was to going to finally get some answers.

Over the following weeks, with the help, support and enthusiasm of Vesna, my trip was arranged. I had flight tickets to Sarajevo booked and she arranged the finer details in readiness for my arrival. Photographs of myself were even sent to Mile in order that he would recognise me at the airport.

Unfortunately, work commitments made it impossible to make the trip of my dreams a lengthy one. Three hundred and sixty pounds sterling obtained flight tickets from Manchester to Sarajevo, transferring once in Munich, Germany.

I would take to the skies at 9am Friday morning, returning to the same runway at 9pm, three days later.

Mam was strongly against my trip, offering on more than one occasion to purchase my tickets from me so that I was at no financial loss if I were to cancel. This further added to my already growing apprehension and I began to wonder if she indeed knew something I did not.

Bosnia had indeed become the old country of scars. Hundreds of years of bitterness and hatred had manifested itself within its diverse inhabitants. Old scores, never settled for long, would always boil over in the cauldron of revenge.

World War II had become the boiling point and would see age-old divisions rise once again. Families would be torn apart or erased completely from history. Ethnic tensions within families would take hold, culminating in murder and betrayal.


Despite my constant drive to uncover the truth, as my departure date neared I began, for the first time, to have serious doubts. Maybe the past should remain the past after all. Terrible scenarios ran through my head. Had Granddad committed some vile atrocity against his own family in a desperate attempt to stay loyal to the cause he had committed to in those dark years of war?

Paranoia and reality merged into one and I could not shake the fear that maybe, just maybe, I was being lured into a game of revenge. If indeed he had acted against his family and then escaped unscathed, living a peaceful life in another country, would it be me, now, who would face the onslaught in his place?

Whatever fears rose within me, I knew the journey must go ahead. The final piece of a twenty-year puzzle was within my grasp and had to be completed whatever the cost.

I would fly to Sarajevo and face whatever consequences awaited me. I had simply gone too far now to give into my own fears and weaknesses.

Whatever the outcome, the truth, for me at least, would finally be revealed.

\* \* \* \*

# Displaced
## Our Lives So Differently Told

## Chapter Ten – The long Road to Brđani

**With everything in place I once again set** off from the dark streets of Featherstone.

This time however, I was alone to face whatever destiny had to offer. I would travel without the company and security of others around me; I would be alone with my doubts and fears.

I had shaken Mam's foreboding from my shoulders and dismissed her repeated appeals and financial rewards for me to turn my back on the search and remain in England; safe in the place I knew and understood.

I had traveled so far now and could not simply turn my back on what I had desired for so long. Despite the fear rising from deep within, I knew I was now at the point of no return.

There is a saying in England,

'You made the bed, now lay in it.'

This certainly rang true as my ever faithful alarm clock announced it was time for me to rise. I had indeed made my bed with my relentless curiosity to uncover what had once been. The final process was upon me and I would not be turning back.

This time the farewells were absent as I loaded my overnight bag into the car and slowly drove away.

Featherstone was silent and in darkness as I made my way past the old haunts of my youth. The bookmakers, or Turf Accountants, where Granddad had been a regular customer, gambling on which horse would win the race, was now derelict in the passing of time. The public houses in which he often drank had said farewell to the last of the revellers some hours before and now seemed to hide within the shadows of the night.

Even the town's cemetery seemed to be darker than usual. I had hated that place so much over the years. First Nana had been lowered into the dank earth and then not twelve months later, Granddad had suffered the same fate. The tree lined path, designed to offer the grieving respite from their sorrows, only exaggerated my own feelings of loss.

The traffic was relatively light on the M62 motorway as it wound itself across the isolated Pennines, the high ridge of limestone peaks regarded as the very backbone of England separating the counties of Yorkshire and Lancashire.

With the high ground now behind me I slowly headed towards the urban sprawl of Manchester and joined the traffic headed to the airport.

Satellite navigation is my own saviour and surprisingly, the car found its own way to its allocated parking space near Terminal One. My own navigation skills are poor to say the least, having gotten myself lost on many occasions. The sexy, almost soothing female voice made no mistakes however and I had arrived at my destination with time to spare.

I had chosen to take the cheaper option of parking just outside the airports perimeter. Local farmers had cashed in when the airport had originally opened and converted agricultural land into sprawling car parks catering for the tide of travellers that were now drawn to the area.

With the car secure in its allotted place I made small talk with the woman whose role was to supervise the days parking schedule as I waited for my lift to the terminal. Excitement overcame me as she asked where I was travelling and I happily told her of my plans. She seemed genuinely interested with the story I had to tell, remarking that maybe I should turn it into a book.

The taxi was prompt and with a final drag on my cigarette I entered the building. I barely remember fumbling my way through everything in my excitement. I do, however, recall stopping at duty free; I bought perfume for Mira and scotch for Mile. Looking back, maybe whiskey was a poor choice to give to a man who distills his very own superior brandy, but my heart was in the choice.

The smoking ban weighed heavily on me there as I waited for my flight to flash its arrival on the departure boards.

God, I so desperately needed a cigarette as I sat waiting for what seemed like an eternity. New legislation had hit smokers hard in England and it was now illegal to smoke in public buildings and spaces and the knock on effect had meant that many public houses and clubs had had to close due to financial pressure. Smoking and drinking go side by side and many now chose to stay at home rather than frequent the ale houses and bars.

Finally, the wait was over. Flight attendants opened the departure desk and I joined the orderly queue waiting to have our passport and boarding tickets checked.

Despite my inner reservations and fears of traveling alone, I remained relatively calm as I boarded the plane.

I was seated with a teenage German girl who spoke more fluent English than I did! Like all counties in the United Kingdom, Yorkshire has its own dialect, often difficult to understand, even for our neighbours in surrounding counties.

The girl, obviously from a wealthy background, was based at a boarding school in England and spent the whole flight talking of her schooling, showing me photographs of her castle-esque place of education. It was obvious her parents were investing heavily for her future success.

Maybe one day she will read this and remember our high altitude conversation. I would not be surprised to one day read of her and her successes.

The short flight passed without problem and we touched down smoothly at Munich airport. Peering out of the tiny window, I gazed down at the sprawling grey runway beneath.

Germany interested me. Twice the country had reared up in its quest for domination of the world, twice it had been beaten back into submission. Germany had been the trigger that would lead me here, seventy years after the first shot was fired. The events of 1939 not only foretold the deaths of countless millions, but had also seen probably as many again suffering the same fate as Maksim. Torn forever from their loved ones, refugees had been scattered across every corner of the world.

Germany also interested me in another way. Granddad had spent time in Displaced People's Camp Zeven, which lay in the British sector of occupied Germany immediately after the war, prior to his eventual arrival in England. It was as if I was now making his journey in reverse.

I had seven hours now until my connecting flight to Sarajevo and so I wandered through the shops looking for nothing in particular, only the passing of time. I felt so terribly alone and craved someone to talk to, I walked aimlessly back and forth, constantly checking the time.

I was also craving nicotine, now having spent six hours without a cigarette. I was still a novice when it came to international travel and was nervous to leave the safe haven of the departure lounge in fear I would become lost and miss the connecting flight. Outside, I felt, was truly out of reach for my ebbing confidence.

The camera flash before me caught my attention. A small crowd of travellers stood taking photographs of a square glass structure in front of them. Curiosity, some say, killed the cat, but I am naturally a very curious person. This time however, curiosity became my saviour.

Like caged animals of intrigue, the glass structure held back not the ferocious tiger, idly eying its unwary prey, but fellow travellers enjoying their much needed fix of nicotine. Munich airport, unlike many others had recognised that smoking, albeit somewhat anti-social, was, after all, an addiction. Meeting the smoker, and the none smoker halfway, the glass structures had been installed, offering the addicts brief respite from the tensions air travel can instill in many of us. Feeling no shame, I eased myself through the snapshot takers and effortlessly slid open the door of the smoker's inner sanctum. The air was cool within the sealed chamber, Fans above, efficiently extracted the polluted air as quickly as it was exhaled. Here the language barrier was insignificant. Smokers united, taking communal pleasure amidst the stares of mystified onlookers.

With my addiction fulfilled I left the safe haven of the smokers commune, careful to take in its exact location, in readiness for my next much needed visit.

Bored now, I settled myself in a seat outside one of the bars. I spent time chatting to a Brazilian guy who was waiting for his own connecting flight home after visiting Italy. We smoked and drank crisp German beer as we made conversation in broken English and the hours slowly drifted by until it was time for a final farewell as I headed for my own departure.

The aircraft was only half booked so I chose to sit alone at the rear. At least here I thought, if something catastrophic was to happen, I would be the last to perish.

The same disillusioned thought had followed me in my career as a coal miner. Whenever I was to descend the vertical shaft I would choose to stand on the upper deck of the man riding lift. If disaster struck on its descent, I would be the last to go.


The hour long flight soon passed and the aircraft dipped its nose to descend. I scanned the dark ground beneath and could make out the clusters of twinkling lights from the houses on the hillsides. Sarajevo was just moments away as the plane rapidly descended.

The realization dawned on me that within minutes I would meet the family Maksim had lost so long ago.

I remembered how lonely he had looked when he was working the land on the allotment. How he had tried so hard to fit into the English way of life, but never quite seemed to get there. It saddened me so much to think that when he had been alone to dwell on his thoughts, he would have been thinking of the people he had lost. With stark realization he would have had to accept he would never see them again.

Now I was to meet his lost loved ones twenty years after he had taken his final dying breath.

My nerves were beating me in the competition to remain calm as I hurried through customs and passport control. I rounded the corner into the arrivals lounge and without having to scan the faces of the people there was instantly drawn to the three figures standing to the left. Mile, Mira and Mile's youngest son, Saša smiled back in recognition.

In awkward embrace we greeted each other. My first impression was that Mile, an imposing figure, was full of tenderness and gentleness despite his visible strength. Mira had eyes which radiated love and warmth as we embraced. She looked so deep into my own that, for a brief instant, it felt as if she was reading my soul.

Saša was vibrant and full of energy, as most teenagers are. He was the English speaker and most of our mirrored greetings were channeled through him.

Maybe I had spent too much time researching the past. Deep down I had perhaps imagined my hosts being dressed in traditional clothing from Bosnia's past. Rough and crudely made clothing more from the era of Granddad than that of today. Instead my welcoming committee could have been taken from any European City. Casual jeans, shirts and jacket had now become the traditional wear for the younger generations of Bosnia.

We slowly made our way out of the terminal building and on to the car park outside. I had been to this place before. Not in person, but as a spectator, watching in awe the daily news footage of the civil war which had devastated this place in years past.

I had seen this same car park, not lined with cars as it was now, but heavily defended by tanks as the city's militia had been besieged and took on the full force of the encircling army in a deadly game of cat and mouse.

I was led to the waiting car. I was living now a truly magical moment. I was amongst the people Maksim had lost. The very people I had searched for so long and, not only was I now in their presence, but they would also lead me to the soil I was so desperate to walk upon.

Despite it only being 11.00pm, the city of Sarajevo seemed deserted. Slowly the car wound its way around the dimly lit streets. Saša eventually broke the eerie silence.

"Andy, our Olympic stadium," he said pointing out of the window to the left.

Through the darkness I could just make out a concrete structure, silhouetted against the night sky. As the car drew closer the true horror of war unfolded before my eyes. The city had been home to the 1984 winter Olympics. Jahorina Mountain had then been the pride of Yugoslavia. Now in the darkness it merely represented the ghost of mans inhumanity towards his own species. Burnt out, deserted hotels and café bars lined the route as the road climbed away from the city.

In the car the conversation was fragmented. We knew little of each others language and Saša at times found it difficult to translate the eager, hurried words.

We headed north away from Sarajevo, rising sharply over serious mountain ridges. These once were the snowy peaks that created idyllic winter scenes for tourists. Now, they were as deserted as the once impressive Olympic Stadium. Ghostly figures of the cable car towers, a monument to what could have been, reared ever skywards. Now the imposing steel structures stood testament to the horrors that had spread across this once beautiful land.

Slowly the road began to dip, bringing with it the pinpricks of flickering lights as we descended toward the town of Novi Travnik. Gradually, the fireflies grew to larger glowing orbs and road signs and houses began to appear along the road.

My first impression of the town was its uniformity. The buildings were set out as if carefully planned. Everything was in square blocks, as if they had been set out on grid lines. The whole town looked to have been set out on a surveyor's desk and left unchanged ever since.

It was only after my visit I read the town had been purposely built to serve the ammunition and armaments factory nearby. Despite the rigours it had endured, Novi Travnik was still impressive to say the least. In its heyday this would certainly have been a town of youth and hope. Gazing out into the darkness I could easily imagine the scenes of yesteryear. Laughter and music filling the streets as Yugoslavia reared its head from the loss and despair World War Two had unleashed. It would have been a time for new beginnings as the then socialist government became hell bent on repairing the countries violent and bloody past, catapulting it into the prosperous days of a new beginning.

Within minutes of entering the town we came to a stop outside a four storey tenement block. This was Mile's home and he gestured for me to follow him out of the car. Like a gentleman, he collected my suitcase and beckoned me to the entrance.

I was drawn to the neatly stacked piles of chopped firewood that adorned the whole buildings facade. As I looked at the neighboring tenements the same piles of wood could be seen. Each building had its own, ready supply of natural fuel. My mind instantly regressed again to Granddads life. He too was obsessed with the need to chop and store wood for burning through the cold winter months.

In his final years this became an obsession and the basement of his house was so full of kindling that it took weeks for us to clear it following his death. To the ordinary eye this may not appear strange, just an old man preparing himself for the winter months. As a retired coalminer however, he had no need to make such efforts to protect himself from the rigours of winter. It was, at that time, the government's duty to provide all coal miners, either still in employment or retired, with free fuel to see them through the winter months. Obviously old habits die hard and he was simply going through the motions of his earlier life. Maybe even reliving the dream of his continued existence there.

I asked Saša about the mountainous piles of wood. In broken, fragmented English he explained the town had been designed with a communal heating system which gave power and heat to every household. During the civil war this had been destroyed by the encircling militia in a direct move to cause suffering to the besieged civilian population. Now with the land at an uneasy peace, the struggling economy could not support the needs of luxury and the heating system was never replaced. Time had been reversed, now the inhabitants were reliving the hardships and rigours their forefathers had experienced so long ago.

Once inside the apartment I was welcomed by Mile's waiting wife Duska, who gestured for me to take a seat on the couch.

Once seated I was offered a small glass of Slivovitz. Not usually a hard liquor drinker I accepted it and, following Mile's lead, gulped it down in one. The clear liquid felt hot as it made its way to my stomach and gave my entire body a deep feeling of inner warmth. Surprisingly I enjoyed its rich taste and eagerly offered the glass for a refill when the bottle appeared again on the table.

Some months earlier I had watched a movie which had been set in Bosnia. In one scene the actors were in the lobby of a hotel and the waiter brought to the table a bottle of the clear plum brandy. As they drank, one of the actors told of the legend that whenever Slivovitz is drunk the devil sits, unnoticed in a corner of the room, laughing. Whether the devil was sat in the room I did not know, or care. All I knew was here I was, surrounded by the kindest people I have been lucky enough to meet and I was being welcomed in a way I will never forget.

The conversation flowed despite the language barrier and photographs of Maksim and Ostoja were exchanged. Although Maksim had been the larger of the two, the physical similarities of brotherhood were obvious. They spoke at length of their Grandfather, his humour, his stubbornness and how he had worked hard all of his life.

Stubbornness was evidently a family trait. Granddad was the most stubborn person I have ever come across. If he declared he was right from the beginning then right he would have to be to the end. I had learned from an early age that no amount of discussion would change his opinion. It was always easier just to go along with what he had suggested.

I recall one manifestation of this stubbornness in particular. He had blamed a workman who was erecting a wall at the top of the street for the dampness that had occurred in his cellar.

No amount of logic could persuade him from his view, so he set out, hammer in hand, to confront the poor man. I remember how I had laughed at the spectacle of the poor workman carefully placing a newly mortared brick, only to have it smashed with a heavy blow from the hammer.

Not wanting to be outdone, the workman replaced the brick only to have this again smashed into fragments. The scene went on and on and when the Police finally arrived the pair were standing amidst a pile of rubble and dust.

Granddad was duly arrested and was taken to the local Police Station. Had it not been for Mam's desperate pleas to the authorities, he would have been charged with criminal damage and placed before the local magistrate for sentencing.

I would later learn from Vesna, Ostoja's granddaughter that Ostoja too had a reckless side to his character just like his brother and his remembered antics continue to amuse the fireside drinking younger generations to this day.

Ostoja, in his prime, had been a keen horseman and had trained one particular horse to, upon hearing his whistle, run from its grazing pasture to kneel in front of the house's front door so as to be mounted. Ostoja had heard that a nearby family was holding a party. Intrigued as to where his own invite was he stepped outside and whistled his trusty mare.

True to form the animal heard its masters call and galloped to the house and kneeled before him. Ostoja rode the few miles to where the celebration was taking place and an altercation, for whatever reason, occurred and he was not allowed entry. Solemnly, he returned home and spent the night thinking of ways to teach the family a lesson they would never forget and to ensure that on any future nights of mirth and merriment they held, he would be accepted with open arms.

Early the following morning he returned to the house and, making sure the occupants had left on their daily chores, set about planting explosives around the doorway. Watching from a safe distance, he ignited the explosives and returned home, happy in the knowledge that for any future parties he would be at the top of their invitation list for fear of his next reprisal!

As the stories and Slivovitz flowed, Mile's wife, Duska quietly busied herself adorning the table with food. I had never seen so much food for so few people! Boiled potatoes, freshly baked bread, salamis, cold meats and the traditional Bosnian dish of Sarma, a dish of meat and rice, mixed together and wrapped in cabbage leaves. Although I had never seen this dish before, I was told by Mam, after my visit, that it had been regularly cooked by Granddad when she had been a child.

The good food, hot liquor, conversation and excellent company only seemed to speed up the passing of time and all too soon it was time to retire. The potent plum brandy had addled my brain to say the least as I clumsily stubbed out the last cigarette of the day.

I was told the next morning would begin at 6am with the hour-long car journey to the village of Brđani.

Tired from the long day of travel and quite intoxicated, I soon drifted into a deep and peaceful sleep.

"Andy! Andy! Time to wake brother," were the words which pulled me slowly from a nostalgic dreams embrace. My eyes slowly focused into the darkness; the child had grown and the dream had gone.

The bear like shadow of Mile standing over the bed erased any trace of sleep from within me.

"Coffee my friend, rise from the bed," he said, more akin to an order this time.

Over coffee I was told there had been a slight change of plan for the day. Mile would not be driving, but he had invited a friend of his to take the wheel and drive me north instead.

Saša would not be traveling with us as originally planned either. This worried me instantly. Despite the terrible hangover, the realisation hit me like a tsunami wave crashing over a beach. Never the optimist, I now feared that I had fallen for the bait and was about to suffer revenge for something I knew nothing about. Saša had been my reassurance. If Mile was planning to settle an old score, surely it would not have been carried out with his son as a witness. Fear gripped me as I realised I may have been right in this assumption. Maybe, just maybe, curiosity had indeed been the slayer of the cat.

* * * *

# Displaced

## Our Lives So Differently Told

## Chapter Eleven - Away into the Uncertain Darkness

**The sweet taste and aroma of** Turkish coffee was all too soon interrupted with the sound of a car tooting its horn outside. I desperately tried to kick start my brain, addled from the hangover of last nights over indulgence. Paranoia was hitting home and, for the first time, I realised I could have made the biggest mistake of my life. I had always been the impatient one, wanting tomorrow to be today. Maybe now this negative virtue of my genetic build up was to be my final downfall.

"Andy," a deep voice snatched me from my thoughts. "It is time."

I was told we should hurry as the journey could be lengthened in the worsening weather.

Outside Mile gestured me into the waiting van which was parked outside. The sight of the van did nothing to lift my spirits. Why a van? Mile had a perfectly good car of his own. My mind was racing. A van was the obvious choice if there was killing to be done. The uncarpeted cargo space in the rear could easily be hosed down, concealing any trace of misdemeanour, suffering or blood.

Mile leant before me and opened the door before gesturing me to take a seat inside. He followed and I sat between the driver and him. Words were exchanged that I had no understanding and the driver smiled in acknowledgement as I picked out the word "Andy" in the quick fire conversation.

"Andy meet my friend Dark," a smile now spreading slowly across Mile's face. I turned to face the driver and forced my own smile of welcome and hello. The name Dark only added to my feelings of fear and hopelessness, but it was the eyes that sent any hope of seeing tomorrow crashing away from me.

Eyes give a lot away to the integrity of the inner person. The eyes that now looked into my own seemed empty and devoid of any compassion. Dark would have been of fighting age during the civil war and would have faced danger, death and suffering on a daily basis. If I now had to choose an ideal candidate for an executioner, Dark would be it. I knew there was to be no escape and today I would face a simple twist of fate. Either Granddad had been the hero I believed or he had left behind a legacy which had never been forgotten, nor could ever be forgiven.

We drove steadily through the town, which appeared to be relatively deserted. The houses and tenements grew fewer in number and I saw for the first time the huge and imposing structure of the Bratstvo Armaments factory. To call it 'huge' is a gross understatement; it was colossal.

Despite having been born and raised within the heavy industries of Yorkshire, I had never seen anything on this scale. This truly must have been the jewel in the crown of the rising socialist Yugoslavia in its time of birth and construction. Amidst the silent scene of dereliction now before me, I could not imagine the factory in its heyday. Like the rest of Bosnia, the civil war had been relentless and without boundary here.

The brotherhood, like the hopes of tomorrow, had slid from reach, leaving only the shattered remnants of what had once been.

Driving steadily on in the darkness and fog, it now appeared such a sad monument to the country's spectacular downfall. It was now nothing more than a broken dream, its Mammoth entirety was lifeless in the steady rot of a decline that had not been triggered by bad management by governing bodies or a world-wide recession, but was the result of mans ability to hate his fellow man. Here stood Bosnia as it was. Years of barbarity, killing and destruction had led to this great monuments demise. It and its people had been bombed out of existence, the factory now left as a tombstone too large to be hidden. Maybe, I thought in sadness, Bratstvo should remain and be preserved to remind mankind what we are capable of and that lessons should be learned and passed on to the next generation in the hope they will not be forced to endure the same fears and loss as the people here had.

Driving onwards we left the sadness of Bratstvo behind and the road steadily climbed into the darkness. As we rose, the fog met with the low lying clouds to add to the uncertainty and gloom now settling deep into my thoughts.

Listening to the barely recognizable conversation going on around me, my mind began to wander back to the possibilities that lay ahead.

With a deep lurch of the heart, I suddenly had the terrible thought that maybe my own stubbornness had taken me here, a step too far. I was no longer in control and had seen the scarred proof Bosnia was indeed capable of anything.

I had been warned countless times to let things be and not to dig into the past. I should have celebrated the life I had known with the man that I revered and not delved into the past he had fought so hard to keep hidden.

Each thought now seemed to accelerate into the next and for one awful moment I accepted here I was to finally meet the fate Maksim had escaped when he left his place.

Was I now to be punished for old scores left unsettled?

The continued secrecy of his life, the death threats on the forums, the attempts to force my rental car from the road during my previous visit all came together in that instant. Even Mam had offered me the price of the airfare to dissuade me from traveling again.

Everything around me now only exaggerated my fear and racing heart. Why a van and not a car? Why the sudden change of plan with the driver? Why?

In the tight confines of the van Mile leant forwards, pushing me slightly to the side as he slowly reached into the inside of his jacket. As our eyes locked, a broad grin spread across his face, made into what appeared a menacing grimace in the darkness.

My mind raced and I suddenly resigned myself to the fact I was in grave danger. It surprised and deeply troubled me just how easily the human mind submitted itself to imminent danger. In those few seconds of uncertainty I weighed up my perilous situation. If I was to breathe my last breaths far from home, I so wanted it to be the gunshot to quickly take away my earthly existence. The knife would bring about a lingering death. Always the coward, I did not want my end to be that of pain and suffering. A quick release somehow now appealed to me so very much.

My wild and irrational thoughts crashed back to reality with the words,

"Andy, Bon Bon?" I looked at Mile's smiling face as he gestured with outstretched hand offering me a boiled sweet. It was if my heart was falling downwards at incredible speed as I slowly held out my own shaking hand towards the offered gift.

I accepted with thanks and sucked on the slightly warming taste of fruits with relish.

Mile offered me the same confectionary at Sarajevo airport on my departure and poured them into my open palm until I could hold no more. These kept me company throughout my return journey and will now be a constant reminder of the kindness that he had shown to me during my initial stay with him and his family.

As my heart rate descended to a more normal pace, the road too swept downwards into a steeply sided river valley which seemed vaguely familiar to me from my previous visit there. We headed north and soon the darkness and fog gave way to daylight. We passed two houses that remained burnt out, relics from the war. These I definitely recognized, as on my previous visit I had used them as a backdrop to a photograph I had taken. Again, an uneasy tension rose within me. I had definitely travelled this route before and knew we were heading in the wrong direction. We were now heading north and not west over the mountain range towards the village we should have been searching for.

The rain worsened, adding only to the confusion as the windows of the van quickly filled with obscuring condensation. I reached across to my right, across Mile's lap to wind down the manual window opener. Mile grabbed my arm with the speed of a venomous snake,

"No window brother, we guard against the cold."

In the gloom we rounded a sharp corner and Mile drew my attention and pointed out to the right. Even in the gloom of early morning the waterfalls at Jajce were a spectacular sight.

At Jajce, the river Pliva meets the river Vrbas and cumulates into a beautiful crescendo of water. It was 30 meters high, but during the war, the area was flooded and the waterfall is now rises only 20 meters. The flooding may have been due to an earthquake or possibly the attacks on the hydroelectric power plant further up the river.

Heading south from Jajce, I noticed for the first time that the road signs were now written in the Cyrillic alphabet. This was a clear indication we had crossed the invisible line from the Bosnian Croat Federation and had entered into the Serbian Republic.

Crossing the invisible border of a country deeply divided in history lifted my spirits and hopes of survival. Surely now we had entered more friendly territory. Granddad had used the Cyrillic alphabet and I now felt as if I was finally on home turf.

The landscape now was familiar. Twelve months previously, I had travelled the same road, only then, heading in the opposite direction. Knowing our adventure had been lost, my parents and I had left the town of Šipovo, heading north, seeking out the safety and comfort of Makarska.

The road now followed the flowing path of the River Pliva. Small settlements could be seen from time to time nestled away on the opposite bank. Smoke slowly rose from the chimneys of the wooden houses, signaling the sleepy inhabitants were readying themselves for another days toil in the surrounding fields.

The river widened as we headed south and quickly became a lake of considerable size. In broken English I was told this was a good place to swim in the summer months and had become a haven for tourists. Regeneration of a broken country was slowly taking form and purpose built rustic hotels and lodges dotted the shores.

"Like you," Mile broke the silence as he pointed out of the vans window.

On the hillside opposite I could make out the huge form of what appeared to be a spoil heap from mine workings. The site was indeed familiar to me and went some way to settling my nerves. 'A little piece of home, so far away,' I thought to myself as we slowly passed by.

"Coal?" I asked with interest.

"Ne," came Mile's reply, "How do you say," he hesitated, trying to form a word I would understand.

"Gypsum," Dark interrupted, "Very old from Turkish rule of our country."

Old memories, previously forgotten, engulfed me as I remembered being a small child sat at the table in Granddad's kitchen. The eggs, as usual, had been perfect, probably having been laid just hours earlier. The soft buttered bread, cut into thin strips or 'soldiers', absorbed the golden yolks as soon as they were dipped inside of the shell.

It had been a Sunday, a day always reserved for play. Like countless generations before me I would make use of the industrial playground that had then dominated Featherstone. Coal production had dominated the landscape for over a hundred years and the waste products of discarded rock and dust scarred the landscape around every mining town. To the children, these were a haven for day long fun and merriment. Here the sterile landscape could be anything a child wanted it to be. Lunar landscape, Everest slope, Sahara Desert, all were within the realms of imagination.

Granddad, surprisingly that day, had allowed the veil of secrecy to slip for a moment. Maybe my own excitement had rubbed off on him, or he had simply wanted someone to share the memories of his childhood with.

He spoke of his own ill spent days as an adolescent. The days he and his beloved brother would hide away bottles of wine and become hopelessly intoxicated as they sat, hidden from view, riding the overhead steel buckets carrying mineral waste onto the hillside. Instinctively I had assumed he had made reference to a nearby coal mine, close to his home. Now as we slowly drove past I stared in total awe. This had been Granddad's industrial playground. His very own place of fun and merriment just as Featherstone, in my youth, had been mine.

Before long we entered the town of Šipovo, the same town that twelve months earlier I had reached and found nothing except hate and the end of my journey. This time however, there were no jeering youths and no aggression to greet us as we drove slowly through the streets, busy with townsfolk despite the early hour and strange, three wheeled tractors pulling trailers of local produce, obviously bound for market.

The van came to a stop and Mile opened the door and stepped out.

"Come brother," gesturing with open arms for me to follow, "Welcome to Šipovo."

\* \* \* \*

# Displaced
## Our Lives So Differently Told

## Chapter Twelve - In the Corner Sat the Devil

Šipovo had suffered heavily in the bloody fight for control in the civil war. Warring factions had almost destroyed the town in their bitter struggle to control the municipality.

Most of the buildings were new and uniform in their appearance as if one person had drawn out the plan, raising the town from the ashes of destruction. In Granddad's lifetime, the growing town would have been much different, merely a small village nestling on the banks of the river. Now Šipovo was a place where old met new. Motor vehicles now shared the roadways with the traditional horse and cart. Denim jeans added colour to the traditional dress of the older generations still clinging to memories of better times and prosperity now lost.

"Come brother," Mile enveloped my shoulders with his arm, "Let us take a drink."

We entered through the door of the nearby bar and were immediately greeted by the owner. The words 'Andy, Maksim and Ćulum' could easily be made out in the quick fire conversation.

"Welcome Andy," the bar owner stepped forwards, embracing me in a tight hug, "I am Slavko and honoured you have traveled so far."

Slavko, on first impressions, appeared to be a mild mannered man, seemingly out of place in the remote town. His English was understandable and he invited the three of us to take a seat near the side door.

He beckoned a waitress, busy cleaning tables in the opposite corner of the room and immediately the table before us was filled with shot glasses of Slivovitz and Turkish coffee.

Although not usually a morning drinker, I followed the example of my companions and drank down the fiery liquid in one. Slavko immediately signalled to the waitress who brought more glasses to the table. This would be the ritual for the next hour.

Although I understood little of the conversation, I could pick out the repeated reference to the name Ćulum and that glasses were repeatedly being raised in obvious toast to the name. Slavko would, whenever possible, try and translate what was being said.

Slowly but surely the effects of the brandy ebbed its way into my brain and acted like its own translator. It was as if I could now understand what was being said in conversation and would nod in agreement when I was being spoken to.

Occasionally we would be joined by others. Despite the calming, almost hypnotic effects of the brandy, some of these visitors sent shivers racing down my spine. I sensed these were not people to upset and accepted their hugs of welcome with submission. Each in turn would take a glass of Slivovitz and toast the name Ćulum before leaving the bar as quickly as they had entered.

Slavko asked if he could drive me to meet his father. Any thoughts of danger ebbed away as the strong brandy numbed by thinking. After all, Mile and Dark would follow us to our destination.

All too soon it was time to move on and bidding farewell to our new found friends in the bar, we departed.

Leaving Šipovo behind the car turned onto a white, chalk track that snaked its way into the surrounding hillside. Slavko spoke a lot as he drove. He had been a very good friend of Ostoja's and knew Granddad had lived out his life in England. Ostoja had told him of the terrible and catastrophic events the day war had erupted into the sleepy hamlet of Brđani. The attacking militia had struck without warning in the middle of the night.

Men, women and children had been targets for their bloodlust and insanity. Those not murdered in the initial attack had been captured and secured in a nearby barn. Cries of mercy fell on deaf ears and the following day the barn had been set alight as waiting gunmen snuffed out the life of any who managed to escape the flames.

Without warning Slavko stopped the car and beckoned me to get out. As I did so I noticed a small stretch of weathered iron railings. There were maybe twenty grave markers dotted about in the rough grass. One of the graves was that of Ostoja, Granddads brother. The same stone marker the kind family had sent me photographs of some months before now laid before me.

Mile and Dark arrived and the four of us stood solemnly around the grave. A candle was lit and we stood offering a moments respectful silence.

"Ostoja's children," Mile broke the silence, pointing to three, crude, hand fashioned stone markers. Their weathered remains made it obvious they had been within the railed confines of the small, private cemetery for a long time. Without wanting to add to the already rising feelings of sadness I asked no questions. Without the need for words I instinctively knew the children, now at rest beneath my feet, had been victims of mans inhumanity and brutality.

With their permission I was able to take photographs of the grave markers, not out of morbidity, but as a lasting reminder I was truly here at last.

The moment of grief passed and we journeyed on along the crude track of loose stone chippings. The scenery, despite the gloom of autumn, was breathtaking. The rolling landscape, carpeted with forests of pine gave way to sprawling mountain slopes rising high into the heavens. How Granddad must have missed this place, I thought.

Slowly rounding a corner I saw for the first time the house. I recognized it instantly from the photographs, but was surprised that it stood alone. I had known the village had been raised to the ground during the attack in 1941, but I had still expected other dwellings to have been erected in their place. The house looked so alone, perched on the hillside and surrounded by the long grass.

"The house of Ostoja," Slavko's words broke the silence, "you will visit there on our return", he continued, slowly driving past.

The rough track carried on, slowly rising before another property came into sight. The house was of a new build, its pink exterior more at home on the coast of the Adriatic than inland Bosnia.

"My house," the pride within Slavko's voice was obvious as he brought the car to a stop. No sooner had we got out, than an elderly man appeared. A brief, quick fire of words was exchanged, including the clear names Maksim, Ostoja and Ćulum. From the broad smile on the man's face it was obvious he was pleased to meet me as he embraced me in warm welcome.

Like the elderly couple I had met on my previous visit, the man before me seemed lost in time. The woolen, sleeveless body warmer had obviously been hand made, with crude leather stitching along the hems. Thick woolen socks stuck out from leather flat soled shoes that could easily have been recreated from the pages of a history book.

Whilst I took stock of the man and the scenery before me, Mile, Dark and Slavko busied themselves in one of the wooden huts forming a rough courtyard in front of the newly built house that was my hosts pride and joy.

Slowly, the three emerged carrying what appeared to be a large, cumbersome object, obviously very heavy as they laboured to negotiate it onto the open ground, scattering the feeding chickens in their path.

Curious as ever, I stepped forward to take a closer look. The alien object was fashioned from copper and had pipes and taps protruding from its sides. Around the base were obvious signs of blackened fire. Although not an expert in home distillation, I knew that this was the top of a fermenting boiler used for creating home made brandy.

The workmanship of the apparatus intrigued me and immediately reminded me of the precision craftsmanship seen on diving helmets from the film *Twenty Thousand Leagues Under the Sea*.

The slowly encroaching chickens once again gave flight as another object was recovered from the sheds dark interior. Made from steel, the cylindrical object stood about one and half metres in height, its bottom half heavily soiled with blackened soot. This was the base that the copper object sat upon. A base which would be filled with crushed plums and boiled for days until fruit became alcohol, its distilled juice released into containers from the copper taps.

The reason for the van and not a car now became obvious. The van had never been meant to be my chariot of suffering and death as I had earlier suspected. It had simply been chosen to carry the bulky load before me from the shed to Mile's hometown, once again to be used for the purpose it had been designed.

With the work done the five of us rested indoors. Again Slivovitz flowed freely. The old man would constantly raise his glass in toast, each time repeating the words,

"Maksim Ćulum, big fish."

Through the steady, but slow translation between father and son, I was given a sketchy glimpse into the horrors Granddad had carried with him for his entire life.

The story had not changed with the passing of time or the divide of distance. First hand accounts had survived and were preserved in an attempt to stop the brutalities of history being repeated.

Militia had attacked the village without warning just as Granddad had recounted. What he had omitted, however, was the brutality and genocide that had followed.

Neither man, woman nor child had been spared. Outnumbered and outgunned, the men had made a desperate stand against the invaders, hoping to give their families time to escape. Heartbreakingly, resistance had been futile and those not killed outright with a bullet were executed as they lay injured and bloody on the ground.

The woman and elderly had fled into the nearby forest, heading for the mountain slopes in a desperate bid to save the children. Escape had never been part of the militia's plan and a deadly game of cat and mouse carried on throughout the night.

Mothers, desperate to protect children, acted as human shields, only to be beaten and stabbed. Mutilated children were left on the slopes before the attackers advanced higher, seeking out more victims ensuring no survivors were left to recount the acts of brutality unleashed upon the innocents.

To the west of the village the last survivors found their path to survival blocked by the slow flowing waters of the river Pliva. The same river, having provided water and a place of fun and mirth, now turned against its own people, cutting them off from their final escape.

Knowing the torture and suffering that was to come, women embraced their loved ones for a final time before lowering them into the flowing water, drowning them so that death was not accompanied with unnecessary pain and suffering at the hands of the merciless militia.

The lucky ones followed their children to a watery grave. The others were captured, beaten and raped before being stabbed to death, their bloodied, lifeless bodies left to rot along the banks of the river which had cut off their escape.

"Time my friends, we have business to do," Mile interrupted my grief ridden thoughts.

A final glass of Slivovitz was toasted before I bade farewell to my hosts and settled back into the company of Mile and Dark for the return journey along the rough stone track.

The swaying motion of the van seemed to reinforce the intoxicating effects of the large amount of brandy I had consumed and I held onto the vans door to steady myself in an attempt to appear sober.

Dark steered the van slowly to the left, braking steadily before switching off the engine.

"Brđani.," Mile announced as he pointed to the wooden house, "You are finally here."

\* \* \* \*

# Displaced
## Our Lives So Differently Told

## Chapter Thirteen – Yesterdays Ghosts

**We left the van and walked** down the grassy slope towards the building that I had only ever dreamed of seeing with my own eyes. Ostoja's home, I had only ever seen in photographs, stood before me at long last. I had reached my destination.

"Like museum Andy," Mile broke the silence. "Very old property," he continued leading the way forwards.

The dampness of the autumn air seemed to exaggerate the feeling of abandonment and despair seemingly radiating from the very earth beneath my feet. Maybe the brandy was playing its tricks as it coursed through my blood; the thought had occurred to me that maybe the devil really was sat laughing in some nearby hidden corner.

This was the very house Granddad's brother had lived in until his death twenty years earlier. Its rustic charm pulsed its way into my soul and, closing my eyes for a second, I felt its atmosphere thick in the air around me. Through a drunken haze of plum brandy and nostalgia, I saw the place as it had once been, not as it stood before me. Children's laughter filled the air as my senses sought out the acrid odour of burning charcoal from the stoves of nearby homesteads. The shrill call of the cockerel pierced the air, announcing to all that he ruled the roost and a new day had begun. The bleating of a lamb, sensing its pending slaughter, broke the spell. The cry for help turning into the creak of old iron hinges slowly giving in to the force pushing past their resistance.

Mile opened the door and gestured for me to enter. The house was much smaller inside than I had imagined. Walking through a narrow passageway, I was surprised just how well constructed it was, despite the quaint crudeness of its exterior. There was one single living room which was adjoined to the sleeping quarters.

An idle wood burning stove sat in the corner and I could imagine the heat and mouth watering aromas that would have been given out in happier times, with family meals being cooked over laughter and conversation.

Although the house had probably not been directly connected to Granddad I could almost feel him there.

He would have known of this house in his youth and what I now saw would have been a familiar sight to him.

Through the large, south facing window, I dwelled on the rolling views across the countryside and imagined him looking out on the scene with his own eyes.

How I wished in that one moment I would have been faster in my search. Four simple letters had kept me from what I sought for so long. The added 'ovic' at the end of the name had thwarted and mislead me over the years and considerably slowed my quest to uncover the truth behind Maksim. The passing of time not only fogs our memories, but also brings about the demise of the very people we search for.

As each year had passed, so too had the knowledge of those who had left us. It was only a matter of time until nothing, not even that beautiful rustic house on the lush hillside of Brđani, would be left to tell the story.

The house was set on a steep slope and from the front seemed to have only one storey. Sloping down to the rear however, it opened up into a two-storey structure. The base was made from rough stone and the upper levels of years old, seasoned, dark timber.

The lower stone section, now dormant, would have had multiple uses in its former days. Tools and everyday equipment that would have been used around the farm would have been stored here. Livestock would have been herded in during the harsh winter months, not only to protect them from the rigours of nature, but also to serve as a primitive form of central heating, giving the occupants above the much needed warmth from the animal's own body heat, rising from the snug below; nature's very own central heating system.

The land around the house was overgrown, nature slowly taking back what was rightfully hers. I followed Mile outside and walked towards the row of plum trees following the rise of the slope.

I was in awe of my surroundings. Bosnia lay before me in all of its beauty. Surrounded by forest clad mountain slopes, my heart pounded as it hit me again that I was finally here in the place I had been searching for twenty years.

It was impossible for me to comprehend that I was seeing for the very first time what Granddad had last seen some sixty years before, before his cruel displacement from the country he had loved so much.

"Stop!" The sudden command jolted me immediately from my thoughts.

Mile grabbed my shoulder in a vice like grip.

"Do not step forward my friend," the Eastern European accent heavy within his voice.

My pulse raced to a crescendo. Bosnia, after all, remained the most densely populated area in the world, not with people, but landmines, forgotten remnants of the civil war.

"Landmine?" I asked, sweat immediately covering my brow.

"Ne comrade," he pointed before me, "dog shit....."

Laughter echoed down along the valley as both Dark and Mile saw the funny side of my fear. Slowly, as blood once again began pumping around my body, I joined in, the alcohol in my system exaggerating the funny side of what had happened.

Despite the approaching onslaught of winter, the sheer freshness and uplifting vigour that the place held was still present and I so wanted to stay there forever, captive in its ambience.

Mile interrupted my thoughts and motioned towards the waiting van. Sadly it was time to leave.

We continued our journey along the chalk white track for maybe five miles and drew to a steady stop alongside a single storey, modern brick house standing in a cluster of similar dwellings.

At the entrance to the house I was met with the smiling and welcoming faces of a man and an elderly woman.

I was immediately ushered inside and offered a seat. No sooner was I seated then the customary shot of plum brandy was offered and by now, readily accepted.

Through struggling with his broken English, Mile introduced the woman as Borka, the daughter of Granddads sister, Sava. Although I had never recalled Granddad ever mentioning a sister, on my return home to England, Mam verified her existence and said that there had in fact been three sisters. The man was then introduced to me as Maksim, Borka's son, named after her uncle, the ever missed brother her own Mam would warmly remember throughout her life.

Through the haze of constant shots of Slivovitz, I remember Borka as if she were sat beside me now as I write this. The eyes and smile were that of Maksim himself and I would constantly be drawn into her gaze like metal to a magnet.

There was a sparkle to her eyes I had not seen for over twenty years and would seem to draw the inner child out of me each and every time our eyes connected.

All too soon it was time to leave the comfort of the little house and with a final farewell and a tear in my eye, I was shown into the car of Maksim, Borka's son.

As before I had no idea where we were headed and with the brandy racing through my brain, nor did I care. I knew now I was amongst the most sincere and welcoming people I had ever met. These were the people who had retained the true human feelings of kindness, the feelings that sadly have been lost to so many of us today.

The day finished in a haze of alcohol, good food and the best company any man could wish for. I was taken to Maksim's home, to meet his wife and children. My recollections there are few as by now the Slivovitz had taken a heavy toll on my senses. I remember the hospitality shown to me and giving out the collection of Euros I had accumulated at Munich airport to the eager children.

My next memory is of being back in Mile's apartment in Novi Travnik. I remember vividly Mira being there and how on meeting for the first time we shed happy tears as we held hands and looked into each other's eyes. The bridge had finally been rebuilt and I had brought Granddad home to the family that he had lost so long ago.

Through the reminiscing, tears and heartfelt stories of an almost forgotten past, my next clear memory is of Mile waking me to say it was time to get ready for the journey back to Sarajevo airport. Maybe the story of the devil and Slivovitz was true after all. In my case, he had waited until the morning of my departure to sit and laugh in the corner. I had the worst hangover possible and my head screamed out each time my thirsty mouth gulped down the offered coffee.

With a sad farewell, I waved goodbye to the kind family who had offered me so much hospitality and settled back into the small car for the journey back to the airport I had landed at just thirty-six hours before.

The journey passed slowly and I was saddened my short stay had come to a close.

The car was small and soon became filled with smoke as both Mile and myself shared one cigarette after another. Repeatedly, I would manually wind down the window in a desperate attempt, not only to breathe, but also to clear the smoke laden air in order to see clearly. Each time Mile would request the window to remain closed and I was relieved when we finally reached our destination.

Sarajevo looked even sadder in the light of day. Graves had been erected everywhere space permitted. Grass verges at the road side, vacant plots of land between scarred buildings, all had been utilised to remember the dead. Sarajevo had suffered and I hoped dearly her days of darkness were behind her, that her people would now move forward and prosper.

At the airport Mile refused to leave until my flight was announced and I made my way through passport control and customs.

In one final gesture of kindness, he beckoned me to hold out my open palm. In doing so he handed me some of the Bon Bons he had offered as we had set out the previous morning on our trip to Brđani. This one simple gesture will stay forever ingrained in my memory as a sign of true kindness that one man can show to another.

Suffering dreadfully from the after effects of spending a full day drinking pure alcohol I wearily made my way to the allotted seat on Flight Lufthansa.

Panic attacks had for years followed me after excessive alcohol use and today had been no different. As the plane steeply climbed upwards from the tarmac I desperately wanted to rise up from the restraints of the seatbelt and force the pilot to abandon his course. Fearing an International flying ban I held my fragmented thoughts together and contained my inner feelings.

Making matters worse for me on an already bad day I had been allocated to sit besides a German gentleman suffering with tourettes syndrome. Tourettes is a cruel condition in its own right. To have someone sat next to you swearing and cursing in a language unknown is another.

Thankfully exhaustion and the bodies inner drive to repair took its toll and deep sleep offered respite from my sufferings.

Twelve hours later I arrived back in Manchester, collected my car and drove home to Featherstone. The trip that had taken twenty years to organise had been and gone in the blink of an eye.

\* \* \* \*

# Displaced
## Our Lives So Differently Told

## Chapter Fourteen – Catching the Coin

**When the coin is tossed, it will** always show the winning side as it stops spinning. Stories too can have a hidden side which sometimes can never be seen unless we scratch at the surface and look closely for the hidden clues offered.

My own story is like the coin, having two sides that were never to be seen together. I would sit and ponder the other side of the story, always wondering what it would be like and sometimes, if the other side ever even existed at all.

Without the strong, unknown pull drawing me to uncover what was there, I would never have found the coins second face. Without this deep desire, the story would never have been there to unfold and to finally understand.

I would spend lazy summer days on Granddads allotment simply staring at the blue sky and imagining being in Yugoslavia. What it was really like there and if the people far away were seeing the same clouds I was looking at.

I would never accept, as others did, that there was nothing there, everyone connected had gone without a trace and the story was lost in the annals of time.

Finally the coin had been tossed, only now it had landed on neither side and instead stood proudly on its axis, showing both sides as if they have always been together, side by side.

The side I had longed for so many years had at long last finally come into view, revealing that my search had not been in vain; my persistence had finally uncovered the truth.

The following pages are like the coin, always having the two faces, but only ever showing one at once. It is impossible for the two faces to ever be viewed at the exact same time and it is a matter of simple physics that gravity will always chose one side to look up to the sky in victory whilst the other lays face down in the earth in despair at being forgotten. At the next spin, the tide may turn and the other side will get its chance to look up at the sky.

In my story, both sides now get to face up. Childhood experiences have combined with reunion to recover the tracks lost to the sands of time. Now Vesna gets to show her side of the story, her face is pointed at the sky and from my story of the mining villages of the North of England, this tale now moves on to a story of hope, academic success and the sheer carnage of a ravaged Bosnia in the hope that this coin will stand upright in defiance and a shared existence.

\* \* \* \*

The Miner's Hostel, Hightown Castleford. Nana is at front, second to the right, Granddad stood, far right.

Taken on a rare holiday in Blackpool, Lancashire. The seaside town was a haven for the working classes escaping the rigours of heavy industry.

Last photograph of Granddad following the birth of my daughter Sasha in 1987. Nana had recently passed away.

A smile to warm a thousand Hearts……..

Final Holiday together. Each year they would spend one week at the retired miners holiday complex in Skegness, Lincolnshire.

Caught unawares. As a child we would often dine out in the nearby Public Houses. Often extremely camera shy Granddad is clearly not amused.

Band of brothers 1. Displaced Yugoslavians enjoying the sun in the grounds of Saville Park, adjacent to the Miner's Hostel. Granddad at front, far right.

Band of brothers 2. Despite the passing of time old comrades keep in touch. I was honoured, as a child, to have been allowed to use the treasured camera.

Petra Markovic (nee Grubač) – Born in 1924. Astonishingly she remembered Granddad living in Brđani before World War Two. She confirmed him being the lost brother of Ostoja Ćulum.

The apparatus used for making plum brandy and the reason why we had traveled into the countryside of Bosnia by van and not by car

Slavko with his father proudly posing for the camera. Both showed me great kindness during my first visit to the village that had eluded me for so long.

Despite having been sent photographs of the house in Brđani finally I would see the structure first hand.

Mile, Borka, Dark and Maksim. Borka was the daughter of Granddads sister and had named her son Maksim after the uncle she had never known.

Mira and Duska continuing the welcome on my return to Novi Travnik from Brđani

Confusion still surrounds these two photographs. Writing on

the back indicates they had been sent by Granddads sister in law from Montenegro and show his wife Stojanka and daughter Zorka. I have yet to trace any side of this family.

# Part Two - Vesna's Story

# Chapter Fifteen - The Other Side of the Coin - Vesna's Story

**Looking back I was so happy** in my childhood despite the suffering of my parents who were simply trying to make the best of the hard times for their children. I will forever look back and thank them dearly for the efforts they made and the sacrifices they have had to endure for our benefit.

My own childhood happiness will be forever enveloped in the love of my sister. Mira is twelve years older than myself and the sort of person you are only ever lucky enough to meet once in your lifetime.

Everyone simply adored my big sister and I remember the feelings of jealousy I always used to feel due to her magnetic popularity, which I now deeply regret.

I remember being six years old when Mom announced she was to leave for work in Germany. Europe was prospering and wages were higher than those of her eastern neighbours.

I recall the utter devastation I felt as she broke the news she would have to leave. Trying to console me, she went onto explain she could make better money there. Offering the child a carrot, she told me that she could then buy me nice things and, with the extra money, life would be so much better for all of us.

With deep sadness and never ending tears, I all too vividly remember even now in my adult years, how the following day she took me to a friend's house where I was to stay while she was gone. I recall the tears of utter devastation I felt and the innocent childish tantrum that was to follow.

I refused totally to stay there and demanded, as best as a six year old can, I should be allowed to stay home alone. Maybe stubbornness is a trait which runs through the blood; rigid it seems, had been my grandfather's middle name.

Mom tried her best, but I guess the debate was simply not negotiable. I would stay at home despite Father working during the day. My brother, Mile would be in school and Mira was away on business in Sarajevo.

The memories from those times remain ingrained in my mind. I can still feel the loneliness and hunger I felt as I sat in the window from 6am as my Father left for work until he returned at 4pm. He would return with milk and crackers which I devoured feverishly. This was to be the pattern for the next four months until Mom returned.

She would tell me for the rest of her life that she deeply regretted the four months she was away. All the money she earned simply went towards paying bills accrued; however, she did bring one thing so special to me which it will stay cherished in my memory forever. It was a little soft dog that would walk and bark. No other kid had a toy like what I now possessed. I was so proud of their envy. I would strut around knowing he was special and everyone was so jealous and desired badly what I had.

I was born and raised in Novi Travnik (New Town) in Bosnia. The area had been built up at the start of 1949 under the directions of Marshal Tito who wanted to turn his vision of an independent, multi-ethnic Yugoslavia into reality.

The town was to house workers for the huge Bratstvo, meaning Brotherhood, armaments factory which, when working at full capacity, would employ more than 11,000 workers.

Marshal Tito had outwitted both the east and western powers in a game of cunning and stealth and now he wanted to show both sides he was capable of defending the unified country he had so proudly created.

It is said the town was such a modern place when it was initially constructed that there was no cemetery for the first ten years. Novi Travnik was affectionately known as "The Town of Youth". Despite its birth into heavy industry, the town remains nestled between the mountain ranges of central Bosnia. Heavily forested mountain slopes plunge down on all sides, offering the respite of nature in the summer months. In the dark, cold days of winter, these were a haven for the more adventurous. Skiing was a favourite pastime for young and old alike.

I remember the games of my youth I would play with Mile. Mile was always master, either his rule or nothing. Whatever game we played he was the King, the ruling party.

I guess, like all older brothers, he was embarrassed of having a little sister who wanted to spend so much time with him. He would tell me to leave him in peace and that I 'was so annoying' when he was around his own friends. Mile would chase me through the house and I would lock myself in the bathroom laughing at his anger.

My Father was a very quiet man and would never say a great deal. Maybe this was attributed to Mom being such a lively, loud person and he thought it perhaps easier to say quiet and refined.

When he did speak however, it would be the words of a wise and knowing man. His advice was so often, if not entirely, the correct advice I would always accept.

He always said everyone should have at least one goal in their life and that his goal was for his three children to successfully complete their schooling.

Looking back to those happy, but hard times, I can now see just how much was sacrificed by my parents to give us three children the very best start in life. A life that would soon be torn apart by bloodlust and war.

Mom was such a beautiful woman both in essence and looks. Her smile would reach out and warm even the darkest of feelings, lifting the spirits of those around her.

Neighbours would comment whenever she went into town the men would cease their daily business and simply stop and stare as she passed. The women would become flustered and annoyed their men folk were so distracted, and could be heard scorning them in annoyance.

Although I was extremely proud of Mom, I was also sometimes a little embarrassed by her. She had the habit of always speaking the truth regardless of what other people would think.

She was courageous and such a brave person, a characteristic that had been moulded as she was growing up by her father, Ostoja, Maksim's lost brother.

She looked up to and adored her father so much. I recall whenever we visited Granddad at his house he would be sat waiting on an old wooden bench outside. I was always intrigued on each visit how she would kneel in front of him and kiss his outstretched hand. Maybe this is some ancient custom from that place. I do not know, but this was how each greeting occurred.

How I loved those days spent at Granddads house in the remote village of Brđani as a little girl. We would always visit in the summer months, the journey during the winter often impossible. I will never forget the smell of freshly cooked eggs and bread that greeted you as you woke in the morning.

Even the mere task of first finding the eggs was exciting to me and I would look with anticipation in the corners and spaces under the house and in the basement where the hens were kept.

The countryside where Granddad lived is breathtakingly beautiful. From the front of the house the view stretches for miles and is only then interrupted by the rising mountains of Gerzovo in the far distance.

The beauty, however, is tinged with sadness and evil. Granddad relayed the same story as told by Maksim. The village had been attacked at the start of World War II. Mom's mother, brothers and sisters had been brutally beaten to death and the buildings burnt to the ground.

Mom, only being a small child would recall witnessing the death of her own mother. Crazed militia attacked, and killed without remorse. Men folk, desperate to protect their families, had been removed with bullets, but women and children could be taken care of without the expense of wasted ammunition. My great-grandmother had been cruelly beaten to death with rifle butts and harsh kicks during the attack.

Left for dead herself, Mom had regained consciousness. Distorted childish imagination took hold of her and she recalled thinking her mother was asleep and how she had desperately wiped away the blood from her body, innocently mistaking this as the remnants of crushed plums, the by product of producing brandy.

To this day I remain saddened no photographs remain of my great-grandmother. Maybe however, as I continue to search out the past, I may be surprised and finally find the image lost so long ago.

I vividly remember on one occasion when we visited Granddad listening to the conversation of the adults. I heard Mom speak of Granddad having a lost brother. This was something completely new to me. I had never heard any mention of a brother before.

Intrigued, I asked Mom about this brother and she reinforced what I had overheard. She said that yes, Granddad did have a brother who had fled to England after World War II and nobody had heard from him since.

They had heard he had attempted to send letters, confirming his survival and continued existence in England. These had been maliciously withheld by the authorities.

From those early days of post war Europe, no one knew where the brother was, whether he had family, or if he still lived.

My first thoughts were that I so wanted to know about him and said out loud he had been so lucky to leave this place. If I were in his position then I too would never return. Granddad looked at me and, tapping his cane in front of him simply nodded his head and said

"Yes, yes, my, brother".


Granddad's little house always felt cosy and warm to me as a child. Grandma always seemed to be busying herself cooking whenever I went to visit. Horrifically widowed, he had remarried during the prosperous years of Yugoslavia's rebirth and regeneration. Despite his domineering nature, Sima held the upper hand. A deeply religious woman, she ruled the house with what seemed like, an iron fist.

For whatever reasons left unknown, Sima left Bosnia in the early 1980's. Living out the final years of her old age within the walled confines of a monastery in Novi Sad, Serbia, where she died.


They lived a very hard life in harsh conditions that felt so crude to me being raised in town. I remember there being no bathroom or shower to bathe and wash in properly. In Andy's account, he recalls Maksim stood by the kitchen sink, washing away the dirt and sweat of a days toil. Old habits perhaps die hard. Maksim now had the luxury of a bathtub, yet he preferred the primitive bowl of water from his own primary socialisation. He continually eschewed the bath and instead used the bowl he had been accustomed to from birth.

\*　\*　\*　\*

# Displaced

## Our Lives So Differently Told

## Chapter Sixteen – Memories of Early Years

**One particular day will stay ingrained** in my memory forever and I recall it as if it were a scene from yesterday.

I was lying down on a blanket at the front of Grandfather's house when I heard approaching voices. A group of elderly people came into view as they walked down the gentle slope towards the house. Curious, I followed them inside and listened to their babbling conversation. One of the elderly ladies asked Grandfather;

"Hey Ostoja have you visited Šipovo recently?"

Granddads reply was simple. "No, why?"

She went onto say that the town was full of teenagers and she could not believe they were kissing openly on benches in broad daylight.

"So ungodly," she said.

"So what is wrong with that?" Came his quick reply. "See these woods around my house, there is not a single tree I haven't had you up against!" With that he simply left the room.

Everyone broke into laughter including me. The elderly woman jumped up so fast as if she had been scolded with hot water, her face turning the brightest of crimson.

That day, like so many others, I remember being sad when it was time to leave and go back home to town.

The way of life there was so different, so slow and lost in time. Just as I was becoming acclimatised to the environment around me and the ways of its people, it would come to a close with the inevitable journey home.

The following days would be filled with an empty air of loss and wanting. I would miss deeply the cosy little house nestled on the hillside, the woods which were mysterious and invited play, the beautiful ice cold water from the wells so pure. Above all else I would miss the sheer tranquillity that enveloped everything and everyone.

It was so good to spend time there with Grandfather and Grandma. In the gentle images of memory I retain of their farewells, I will always see Grandfather standing at the front of the house, tapping his cane between his feet as Grandma hugged me tight, tears in her eyes as she whispered "My cherry pie, I will miss you."

Mom would cry too as we left and I would always wonder if we would ever see them again.

As a teenager, it was always important for me to visit Grandfather. By doing so it felt like I was staying in touch with my roots and reality.

In Novi Travnik, the whole hippy revival was in full swing and I was being drawn into this as most teenagers do when following the influence of their peers.

My sister, the ever loving, but suspicious mentor, kept a close reign on me, so worried that I would fall into the drug culture which raised its ugly head along with the music and fashions.

Looking back fondly, those carefree days were probably the best moments of my life. We lived under the ever-watchful eye of socialism, crime was almost non-existent and everyone seemed to live together in peace and harmony.

Despite the death of Josip Broz (Tito) in 1980, Yugoslavia, for me, was a place of prosperity and harmony. Maybe I was naïve, or simply too young to understand the consequences that Tito's death was to wreak on the unified country I knew and loved.

In those carefree hippy, happy days, I could never have imagined the horror which was about to envelope the country,

Old wounds were soon to open, divisions between my people would manifest once again and fate would be sealed for thousands who would never again see tomorrow.


As adults we often think back to the happy times from our younger days and I recall, although happy and full of energy, I always dreamed that one day I would spread my wings and leave the place I knew so well.

I would look up to the sky and my mind always wandered into the hazy realms of my imagination. I always tried to visualise the family who were possibly in England.

I knew Grandfather had a brother, Maksim and I wished to know more of his fate.

With this lack of knowledge I always felt incomplete, as if my very essence had been removed and dissected, being replaced with an inner emptiness. It was as if I was missing something so very important from my inner self.

Like all teenagers, I would at times find myself in conflict with my parents and would lay awake at night wishing so dearly to uncover the whereabouts of Maksim. How I wanted to find him, to tell him I was here and longing to move far from this place. With dread I knew this was not possible and was saddened to think the same thoughts were possibly being mirrored by someone unknown in England.

Little did I know back then that at the same time there was indeed someone starting to scratch at the surface of this story.

The scratching would continue for another twenty years and would eventually lift the guarded veil which had been secret keeper for so long. The tossed coin would finally settle at last onto the ground, this time however, both of its sides would be in view of the other.

Although the dreams of being taken from this place never came true, I continued to live the happy, carefree life of a kid at school.

I had visions of becoming an interpreter and pursued my knowledge of the English language hoping this would give me a good start in life. English is widely used all over the world.

Unfortunately my parents did not agree and my high hopes of enrolling at college were stopped in their tracks when they announced they could not afford the tuition fees.

The only alternative for me was to try and get a scholarship. The only academy available for such a scholarship, however, was the military academy in Zagreb, Croatia. My sister, whom I looked up to for inspiration, encouraged me to follow this direction, but I was faced with a problem that I would first have to overcome before I could qualify for this help.

Because I had all my hopes pinned on becoming an English interpreter I had not focused any attention on the subject of mathematics. This was needed in the academy, so I was to spend the next two years studying in order to gain a satisfactory grade. Soon, studying became my obsession and I would seldom leave the house to socialise like the other teenagers in town. Instead I would tirelessly read endless mathematics books and prepare myself for the final exam that would give me the golden ticket and allow me to enter the academy in Zagreb.

Those two years seemed like a living hell to me. I would see and hear the other kids having fun whilst I busied myself with textbooks. Friends I had known for years started to avoid me. Now they saw me as being boring and very different to them.

I would constantly worry myself with thoughts all of this may be for nothing and that, maybe I would not even pass the examination and all of my efforts would be wasted.

I look back now and regret during those two years I missed out on spending more time visiting my Grandfather at the house I adored so much. That place has a special spot in my heart. It is like a lost world which is cut off from the rigours of everyday life. Nature in the area is everywhere and seems to fill everything with its freshness. It reaches into the soul and draws you in to its tranquillity. I would often lie in the grass near to the house at night and stare into the clear sky at the countless stars that twinkled and winked in response to my gaze. It was always as if the sky there had more stars than anywhere else on the planet. I felt privileged to marvel at the spectacular sight.

Thankfully, the relentless studying paid off for me and I passed the exam and was able to enrol at the college in Zagreb.

Maybe this would never have been possible without the constant and unrestrained support my sister gave me during those seemingly never-ending two years and I will always feel that I owe her so much.

Before I left for college, she took me on a short holiday to a hotel perched high in the mountains. She knew that I felt so connected to nature and this would be the most perfect of places to take her little sister. She knew I would adore it.

I remember the feeling of freedom and liberation from my studies and was in total awe of the spectacular location in the mountains. The whole place felt so untamed and far away from the hustle and bustle of our modern lifestyle. The air, the grass, the rivers, all lifted my spirits to a new found high and I felt intoxicated in the natural, untouched beauty engulfing me from every direction.

Zagreb is without doubt the most beautiful city in the entire former Yugoslavia.

The lifestyle there is carefree and easy going, a far cry from the strict regime of the military academy I had entered into.

The day there would start at 7am with breakfast. The Mayor would examine beds each morning and then we would be drafted into our various lessons that commenced at 8am. Lessons would continue until 3pm and then it would be a forty-minute train and then bus journey to the hostel I was lodging in.

There we would eat and try to relax a little before the return journey for lessons that ran from 4pm till close at 7pm. I would return wearily to the hostel and continue with online studies well into the night.

Because it was a military academy it was run with a strict military regime. At times it felt more like a hardcore prison than a college. I would often lay awake at night wandering just what I had let myself in for.

The weekends were my release from the strict and uncompromising torture I was enduring and I would venture into the very heart of the city.

Other students from Bosnia were there and we would meet, drink and party. Those weekends evened out the daily rigours of college life and made life there a little more tolerable.

Although I felt I was being pushed to my very limits under the harsh regime, the years seemed to glide past and I soon found myself in my third year.

Every Friday I would receive money from Dad with the same message he had been writing from the very first week,

"Be good and study. Love you, Dad".

Fridays were always the happiest day for me. Those words meant so much as I loved my parents dearly and missed them so much.

When you are young and happy you never really think anything can shatter your dreams and plunge you into despair.

Everything was so easy and natural and we were without a care in the world. We had music and fun. Pink Floyd, Janis Joplin and Jimmy Hendrix were the gods we looked to for inspiration. We would have concerts, play guitars and above all else, have laughter in our lives.

It felt like I was in the heaven the biblical books wrote about and like most teenagers, I never questioned if this would ever come to an end.

Pink Floyd wrote,

"Now there's a look in your eyes, like black holes in the sky". My own black hole came the day I was jolted back into reality.

I was told Grandfather had died after a short illness. I could not take this in and thought over and over that no, there was some mistake. He could not die, he would live for ever because that was the sort of figure he was. Ostoja, to me, was an immortal man who would never die. He was a rock, old and reliable; he would be around forever. He had suffered so much in his life and I always believed no illness could ever take him away.

As the days slowly passed it sank in that, yes, he was dead and I remember the utter feelings of guilt and remorse which engulfed me.

I felt helpless and so selfish I had not visited him in four years. He had died in the harsh environment of Brđani whilst I was here, enjoying life, so carefree, lost in my own world of laughter, music and happiness.

I was told of his demise seven days after his death and after the funeral. My family thought this was the best way, as they did not want my schooling to suffer if I took time out to travel home to Bosnia.

At night I would lie awake and until I eventually cried myself to sleep. Tears would flow in a never ending stream of sorrow. I remember thinking that I would never again be the subject of his wise and knowing advice, nor his addictive laughter and jokes.

I was constantly drawn back to my last visit to that beautiful place. He called out as he saw me approach,

"Hey Petra you came, did you bring me lamb meat?" I answered no it was not Mom but me.

"Oh it is you Vesna, my sun you are." Those are the last words I remember him saying to me.

It is so ironic that within twelve months the other side of this coin would feel the same sorrow and utter devastation with the loss of Granddads brother. Here began the emptiness, the catalyst for a twenty-year search for understanding.

Although my own sorrow at losing Grandfather was intense, I felt dearly for Mom. She loved her father with a passion. He was the only surviving family member that had escaped the night of horror back in 1941. Although he had remarried, Mom and her step- mother Sima, never really came to terms with each other and probably only ever tolerated each other through the love of the same man.

Sima was a deeply religious woman and often invited elderly priests to stay at the house. With her it was simply gods way or no way.

After his death they only met to exchange monies that Mom had secured to purchase Grandfather's property and land.

With that sealed, they would not cross paths again. Sima, having no reason to stay now in Brđani, moved on.

Following the death of Grandfather, I was again drawn to the lost brother and wondered of his fate. Was he still living? If he was, did he know his own brother had died?

My sister would recall whenever Mom asked her father about his brother Maksim, he would struggle for breath, tears would well upon his face and he would make his excuses before hurriedly leaving the room. It was obvious in this case, the passing of time had not been a healer and he clearly missed the brother who had long since departed.

Back at the academy, I was beginning to enjoy the constant regime of learning. In my final year the pieces were beginning to fall into place and I now felt I was at last achieving something.

I remember the visits to family in Bosnia, especially those visits to my brother. He would coax me and joke that I was the smart engineer of the family. He would fire mathematical questions at me and I was always frightened my answers would be incorrect, as he too had spent some time at mechanical school.

Finally my school days came to an end with my graduation. I will never forget seeing my sister who had come to take me home; an acoustic guitar, wrapped in a huge bow was her present to me. I wept with sheer joy at the sight of the gift and we held each other and cried for what seemed like an eternity.

\* \* \* \*

# Displaced

## Our Lives So Differently Told

## Chapter Seventeen - Bratstvo – Welcome to the Machine

**It was so hard for me** to say a final farewell to the people I had grown to love during those long years at the academy, but regrettably, it was finally time for me to leave and return to my hometown in Bosnia.

Zagreb will stay ingrained in my memories forever. Like a beautiful companion that had helped me through the strict and disciplined regime I had to follow throughout my studies.

The journey through the mountains passed quickly and I felt the realisation hit that I was now to face the tough transition into 'real life'. I had to go from a carefree student, idling away the summer weekends, to a working adult with the responsibilities such a role brings.

It was only when I finally arrived home that I realised just how much I had missed my family. Evenings were spent chatting and catching up on missed moments from when I had been away. Mom I remember, would sit and smile as I caught her gazing lovingly at me. It felt as if she was seeing me for the very first time and would embrace me tight to her chest, as if never wanting her baby to leave again.

After seven years of dedication to study, I was happy to stay embraced in the love of a family I had missed so much.

This, I feared was not to be for long and I was expected to report for work at the armament factory situated on the outskirts of town.

The factory was colossal in size and employed between seven and eight thousand workers. The reality of my new situation hit me hard as I entered through the huge gates on my very first day.

I had expected a reward of some kind after my strenuous efforts with my education. Instead, I felt hugely disappointed. I was herded into the huge workshop with hundreds of others starting the day's work. I felt like an ant in a colony as I looked into the tired faces of those already used to the daily grind.

Most of these faces I recognised from town and I was welcomed aboard with kind smiles. I would smile back as the eager newcomer, but deep down I was already having regrets that I had entered such a place.

Maybe, I thought, the life of an engineer was not for me despite the tremendous efforts and time I had given to pass my grades and make it here.

Despite my inner reservations, I held my head high with pride and worked with the feverish pace and enthusiasm of youth.

Maybe my enthusiasm was to be my downfall, as I was moved to the largest of the workshops where I would carryout computerised diagnostic testing on the huge machinery there. Although proud that I had been selected so early in my career at the factory, I was also having the feelings of suspicion and dread. Mira, a friend at the factory, would laugh and wish me good luck; she said this with a knowing smile which began to disturb me as if she knew what was awaiting me there.

I remember feeling desolate isolation as I entered the workshop that very first day. To say it was huge would be an understatement. Thousands of faces seemed to turn and look at me in unison. The shouting and whistling rose to a fever pitch as I wearily walked down the long aisle of clattering machinery. The air was warm and tinged with the odours of sweat and oil.

The whistling and shouting continued without relent and I felt so very alone and out of my depth. I was ushered into the foreman's office and was told to ignore the mayhem around me.

The leader then took me back onto the shop floor, the shouting grew in decibels and I turned to see in horror one of the workers had picked up a tool and was posed as if to strike the worker next to him. In sheer panic and fear I turned and ran towards the very same door I had entered only moments earlier.

I realised in that instant I could not stay at the factory, the people there were maybe a little crazy and I feared it would only be a matter of time before behaviour like that which I had just witnessed would ultimately lead into someone receiving a serious injury, or worse, at the hands of the mob.

I remember going home that night, so frightened and alone, my heart in mouth and so very confused.

With fear and dread, I would return to the mayhem and chaos each day, never understanding the scene now being played out before me.

Each day I entered the workshop and the cackles and whistles would slowly falter, something far more important than me was about to enfold. Everyone was guessing, speculating what was going on. The stories were varied and ranged from politics to trading, but nobody really knew what was actually about to happen.

With a heavy heart, I knew I was slowly turning into one of the jostling faces at the factory.

Although I had studied for so long to become an engineer, my heart simply was not in it and I yearned for something more. I fought desperately against the desire to leave the factory. Eventually, however, its pull was too strong and I gave in and started to think of alternatives.

I would think of the family possibly existing somewhere in England and so wished somehow, after all these years, there would be a connection.

Despite my wishes, the years slowly passed and I truly became, without realisation, one of the oily faces from my nightmare first day at the factory.

Three years passed before I awoke from the slumber of routine that I had fallen into. I awoke feeling dread at who and what I had become. I realised that now I really had to escape this place and began to plan my future away from the grimy existence the factory offered. I even allowed myself to think of leaving Bosnia.

My parents realised just how serious I was when I told them I was going to apply for a visa and head to Switzerland where I was to stay initially with family friends who lived there.

\* \* \* \*

# Displaced

## Our Lives So Differently Told

## Chapter Eighteen - Did You See the Frightened Ones?

**Maybe Mom and Dad also recognised** that something was stirring in Yugoslavia and it would be a wise decision for me to leave. The economy was in a nosedive and people were out of work like never before. Rumours began to spread Yugoslavia was now beginning to spiral into economic disaster. The National Debt soared almost as quickly as the number of the unemployed. First Slovenia and then Croatia announced they were ready to break away from the once mighty socialist unity of the republic. Tensions were rising and perhaps my parents, survivors of the darkest days of World War II, knew all too well the fate that was to await the once great state.

I applied for a four month visa and busied myself packing and looking closely at my options. Despite the strenuous efforts I had made to qualify as an engineer, the truth was that I was not committed to this as my life long career and, even worse, I did not truly know what it was I wanted in life.

In Switzerland again, the impatience of youth took control and I was becoming homesick. Despite the excitement of my new surroundings, I desperately waited for the day I was due to return. I felt like an outsider in a country foreign to me and deeply missed the comfort of home.

In the final weeks of my stay, I finally began to listen to the conversations and the stories being told in the bars at night.

They centred on a widening rift between the Serbian and Croatian people that was worsening daily. Croatia had openly announced it wanted to break away from Yugoslavia. Serbia was strongly opposing any move towards independence. People were advising me not to return to Bosnia and I should instead be looking for other alternatives.

Maybe my stubbornness got the better of me, but I put these stories to the back of my mind and returned, without any thought, to my hometown of Novi Travnik.

I remember walking through the town I had been raised in and knew so well. In the short space of my four month absence something there had changed; something was unfolding I had no understanding of. Everyone seemed to be in a great hurry to complete their daily business and quickly return to the relative safety of home.

The stories of mayhem were countless and I remember feeling frightened and for the first time in my life, so very alone. I was just one small person, standing in the middle of something so huge. I would ask what was happening, but people would simply look at me as if I was from another planet.

Even my family were acting strangely. I would overhear them in hushed conversation in the evenings. The talk always centred on the worsening problems between the Croatian and Serbian people. The economy was spiralling out of control in Bosnia and the only way forward was for ordinary people to look towards the private market for employment and not to rely on the state controlled industries for security, as had been the case under the old socialist federation. For the younger generations this idea seemed ludicrous. Born under a successful socialist regime, we knew nothing of capitalism or the private sectors of industry. To simply dismiss socialism was not an option we could follow. Socialism had raised us and made us who we were.

As the talk and speculation grew in intensity, I received a telephone call from my sister Mira. She had lost her job in the never ending stream of unemployment. Mira warned me that things were only to become worse in the weeks to follow.

She went on to say all businesses in the surrounding areas were turning to the private sector and we too had no alternative, but to follow down the same route. She was adamant that for the family to survive the impending chaos, we would have to look at investing the money we had into a private enterprise and the best option open to us, given the limited investment available, was to rent a suitable building where we could operate a wholesale and retail store for cheap and affordable clothing. After all, despite the worsening economic climate, people would always need shirts on their backs.

The following few months saw Mira's advice turn into reality. We pulled together our resources as a family and secured a suitable address in which to operate. The days were excruciating long and hard, but eventually we found ourselves making slow headway in the rapid transition from socialism to capitalism.

Although the stories were now of open warfare on the Croatian – Serbian border we put these thoughts to the back of our minds and focused all of our efforts on making our small family enterprise a success. After all, the border was distant and we wrongly, in hindsight, thought the fighting would not affect us in Bosnia.

Following the initial enthusiasm and progress made, we soon found it increasingly difficult to find a ready market on our doorstep, yet we needed consistent sales to provide us with enough income to allow us to continue trading.

While others around us were failing, we were forced to travel around to find buyers for our wares. It became a tortuous ritual of travel and sell. The days were never ending as we covered the markets from Belgrade to Zagreb. We would simply drive through the night and promote our goods during the day. It was a repetitive, exhausting cycle that we had to pursue in order to survive.

As the days passed, fighting became more widespread in Croatia. All-out warfare soon erupted and it was as if the world had turned its back on our plight.

With the desire to keep our heads above water burning bright, we carried on the daily ritual of work, work, work and became oblivious to the danger was settling in all around us.

Fierce fighting was widespread on the border regions, the same borders which had been invisible since 1945.

Despite the ever-tightening envelope of financial survival we had surrounded ourselves in, it was slowly dawning on us we were not as immune to the tensions rapidly escalating in our country as we had hoped.

As days passed it was all too apparent that the civilian traffic on the roads was dwindling, to be replaced by the sheer might of military hardware. The tank was replacing the car and it was obvious to all something huge and horrific was about to happen.

One night in particular brought reality crashing down around us and left us in no doubt that our tiny enterprise was nothing compared to what was about to be unleashed upon us all.

As was the usual for our accustomed routine, we were driving through the night to a new location so we might find another market for our wares. The road, which cut through dense woodland, was particularly dark. Rounding a sharp corner we were forced to swerve sharply to avoid a military roadblock. The car came to a shuddering halt and we were faced with the formidable sight of a huge armoured tank within inches of our own puny mode of transport. A close collision, in the dead of night with a M-84 battle tank, weighing in at a mighty 41.5 tonnes, would have been traumatic to even a battle-hardened soldier. Given the David and Goliath comparison, it was in no ones doubt who would have been the winner had there been an outright collision between the two.

In blind panic we tried in desperation to turn the car around and were immediately halted by the sharp order to stop by a military figure, pistol in hand, illuminated in the cars headlamps.

He ordered us to get out of the car and asked where we were headed. We explained we were driving to Belgrade in order to trade there. The soldier looked at us in sheer amazement as if we were crazy. With a shrug of his broad shoulders he waved for us to return to our car, turning round with a final shake of his head.

Realisation was dawning on me that the idle conversations and tales of dread we had been hearing had truth to them. The dark shadow of death was settling over this land and we had naively placed ourselves right within its icy grasp.

Evil was moving slowly, but surely across Bosnia and its spread could not be stopped. Within weeks of that sobering encounter in the woods, Novi Travnik was slowly being sucked into the impending dark abyss. The devil had once again come to visit. He would not be sat in the corner laughing as brandy flowed though. This time he was bringing death and suffering to wreak havoc upon us in mighty vengeance.

Strangers began to arrive in town with hate in their eyes as they glared, scanning everywhere and everyone.

I would hurry through the streets in fear of the newcomers and would not venture out after dark. Others felt this too and I remember listening through the apartment window, hearing only the echoes of empty, deserted streets. These same streets, only months before, had been filled with children, footsteps and laughter.

Occasionally I would be woken with a start in the early hours to the sound of shouting and the violent banging on neighbours doors. Gunshots would be heard and the stories of robbery, violent beatings and rape were becoming more and more frequent. The strangers with hate in their eyes had now become law and master to the town's fearful inhabitants. They could do as they pleased and no one could stop them. With this knowledge, the horrors worsened, even daylight was no longer a welcoming sight, as it did not bring any respite from the fear and dread of nightfall.

Soon, even worse news began to filter its way through to us. Open warfare had spilled into Sarajevo. Worse still, civilians were being targeted and the horrific details of mass murder and mutilation were countless.

Poor Sarajevo, a place of multi-cultural cohesion, was now being turned into a bloodbath of hate and indifference. Diversity had been placed into a pot and now the pot began to boil.

Even my own town was becoming a breeding ground of hatred and revenge. It was as if a great plague of inhumanity was being spread amongst neighbours that had lived side by side in relative harmony for decades. Old, almost forgotten divisions once again reared their ugly heads, turning man against man, woman against woman and child against child.

I have never felt fear like I felt at that moment and so desperately wanted to leave the horrors and barbarity behind.

Again my thoughts turned to those of Grandfather's brother in the safety and luxury, of England. If only we knew of family still living there, maybe we could reach them and flee to safety. Even with the naivety of youth I could see all too clearly now that we were in terrible danger with no hope of escape and salvation.

Hatred would rear its head constantly and neighbours, friends and even families would be torn apart by its vile presence. People who had loved each other mere months ago would now attack, maim and even kill their newfound enemies.

Horrors became just another part of everyday life and people would simply look in the other direction when scurrying through the streets. Law and order had deserted the people and in it's place stood mob law.

Refugees from Sarajevo flooded into the town and the whole place looked as if were a casting call for extras in a Hollywood war movie. The scene before me was unreal and I would shake my head as if to rouse myself back into reality.

The refugees would speak of horrors they had witnessed first hand. They told of the city being totally cut off from the outside world. Of artillery and mortar attacks that were being aimed at the thriving market places where civilians packed into to try and buy the dwindling food stocks to feed their hungry families. They had made it out just in time before the final escape routes had been sealed and the people who now remained there were helpless to defend themselves against the vicious onslaught. Now their fate had been sealed and it was no longer a case of if, but when they would die.

Within days of the first refugee influx, a convoy of buses arrived in town. The passengers were packed tightly and they were all children. Their faces looked out with unimaginable despair. They looked empty and completely devoid of hope. They were the children of Sarajevo. Their parents had remained, condemned to their obvious demise within the city.

Everyone crowded the buses to take the children to the safety of their homes. I embraced a brother and sister. We cried so much as we held each other so tight. We gave them food and shelter overnight before they continued their own sad and harrowing journey to safety. It was so dreadful to think, as you looked into those helpless and innocent eyes that most, if not all, were already orphans.

The next morning was so sad to see the children being returned to the convoy and heartbreaking to watch them wave as they were driven out of town.

I later learnt with great sadness the convoy never reached its destination and the vehicles were never to be seen again. Maybe that night of respite in our town had been their last. Rumours circulated the convoy had been stopped and redirected into the woods. Without compassion, it is said, the buses had been torched with the innocents locked inside. Those lucky to escape the flames had been brutally gunned down by a wave of machine gun fire. Maybe one day, the mass graves will be discovered and the truth of the missing children will finally be told. Then they will be laid to rest where their surviving families can finally come together and grieve.

\* \* \* \*

# Displaced

## Our Lives So Differently Told

## Chapter Nineteen - Switching off Humanity

**I look back now and it** amazes me how the human mind can adapt itself to the situations it finds itself in. There I was, struggling daily with my own survival, whilst witnessing the horrors and horrendous brutality which played out around me every second of every day.

Every vile and inhuman act of savagery I would seal away in the back of my mind as if it had never happened. I knew that to survive, I had to remain strong and continue to just simply function in a world of no hope. Sometimes, it became a struggle to hide away the terrible images we were baring witness too and the struggle to keep the secrets would add to the immense weight we carried on our shoulders. To survive, you had to revert to primeval instinct and it was that which would carry me through the next four years of warfare and sacrifice.

I remember one day in particular, I had ventured outdoors to visit a friend who lived nearby. As we chatted in her apartment, we began to hear footsteps and raised voices coming from the town square below. Curious we stepped onto the balcony to see what was happening. We were met with the spectacle of soldiers in black uniforms standing in rows. At the forefront was their commander who was bellowing orders. Although I could not hear what was being spoken, I knew by the response of the black uniformed audience it was not a Sunday sermon. They would yell and whistle in agreement and, as the crescendo reached fever pitch, they began to fire their weapons into the air. This was not some spaghetti western being played out, where the Mexican bandits celebrated victory with sporadic firing into the cloudless skies. This was Novi Travnik and the world had deserted us.

In panic and desperation we ran from the balcony into the apartment, closing and locking the door as if this simple act would keep us safe from the anarchic scene below. We stayed there huddled together in prayer and, as darkness fell, the nightmare began.

Outside we could hear the heavy footfalls of a stampede. The footsteps became louder and we knew they were coming from in front of the apartment block. Then came the frightening thunder of gunfire and the deafening explosions that rattled the very foundations of the building.

I remember the feeling of utter terror when the realisation dawned that open warfare had arrived on the streets of my hometown. I wanted to crawl away and hide, but realised I was trapped right in the middle of the carnage and murder. Sounds of breaking glass resounded from below and I knew that apartments were being trashed by the unknown assailants. The scene repeated itself throughout the night, running footsteps, shattering glass, gunfire and the screams chilled the soul.

Although I am not naturally a religious person, I sat in that small room and prayed like I had never prayed before. Waiting to die is a feeling never to be explained. How the condemned must feel waiting for the gallows or the electric chair became clear to me as I waited for my own end to come. I had read once of English nobility paying their executioners to provide a quick and painless end. How I wished, hiding there in the dark, that I had a fortune to offer to my executioner when he battered down the door.

Each second passed by slowly and as daybreak beckoned, the noises gradually lessened and eventually broke into and eerie silence. Whether the attackers had grown tired of their murderous hunt, or they had simply run out of innocents to butcher, I do not know. I was spared and my own life would continue.

I remember the scenes of destruction as I ran through the empty streets to reach my family's apartment. Buildings were burning and the stench clawed at my nostrils. I was fighting for breath. but my legs refused to give in to exhaustion. Before I knew anything else, I was home and leaping into my Mom's open arms, still struggling for breath, now battling to hold off the sobs that would rack my already exhausted body.

That night was just the beginning of the fresh horrors which were to become a daily scene of murder and survival. I so desperately wanted to escape the living hell, but there was no way out. I realised that returning to my homeland had been a grave mistake and I was now destined to face the consequences, however terrible they may be.

Humanitarian organisations set up shelters all across town and offered food rations. I would watch the faceless queue with tears of sorrow and pity at our shared situation. Each day I would notice the absence of somebody else I knew. Each and every time I would fear the worst.

Absent friends had now become merely a statistic in this abject chaos.

Like those around me I had become merely a face in a desperate crowd. I would remember the Pink Floyd video *The Wall*. The lifeless masks were now being worn by all those around me and slowly I began to wear my own.

At night I would lay awake and cry myself through the long hours. Everything I cherished had gone; the beauty that had once surrounded me in this town had slowly sunk into rot and decay, as I stood helpless against the tsunami of evil which had finally breached the shore of humanity.

Loneliness is probably one of the hardest crosses we can bear. One of the deepest and strongest human emotions is to feel the need to belong and to be a part of society.

One of the worst things that can happen is for us to be rejected by the same society which had created us.

I remember the feelings of utter and total despair when this happened to my own family and me. It was as if we simply no longer belonged amongst those we knew so well and the surroundings to which we were accustomed.

We had suddenly lost all of our self worth and were left merely to hope one day we would again find our place amongst our neighbours.

Mira never gave up hope of saving the family from the chaos and destruction. Bravely, she once again packed the car with clothing and set off, with her then husband Darko, attempting to break the siege and reach nearby villages. Money now meant food and she risked all to feed her family.

Under the cover of darkness she had found a way out from under the ever-watchful gaze of the snipers. Driving without headlights to avoid detection, they arrived in a nearby village as dawn was breaking.

Sporadic gun and mortar fire filled the air, but in desperation they continued through the derelict streets until brick and stone blocked their path. Before they could even begin to ponder their next move, heavy, fast paced footsteps could be heard within the smoke riddled ruins. The footsteps faltered in front of their car and a thud resounded on the metal work immediately in front of the windscreen.

Footsteps and smoke gave way to the horror now Mira had to witness. The decapitated head stared lifelessly at her. His brutal end etched forever in his wide, open eyes.

I was learning so fast how hatred can spread its vile web into the very core of the human body and soul. How religion and language can manifest itself into a reason to kill and torture.

I would see daily how older, respected individuals would feed this vile hatred into the minds of the younger ones. Gullible, open-minded youths who would kill and maim for a cause they had been so heinously misled about.

I look back and think of those people that brought so much bloodlust and carnage to the ordinary folk and I wonder if they ever ask themselves the simple question of why? Do they have remorse for their actions? Do they carry the heavy burden of their part in it all?

With the chance to make life a little more bearable and no other options, I returned to work at the armaments factory. There was little else left now in the town and at least the sporadic wages would help ease the pain of day to day living.

We assembled at the factory gates at 7am and silently prayed that the same flag as the day before would be fluttering in the breeze as it came into view. Often, it was not, which meant that a different warring faction had taken control of the area during the previous nights battle.

Each day, the workforce was rapidly diminishing in number. It was not a gradual decrease, but a sudden drop of a hundred people or more as all manner of horrific stories were being relayed on the shop floors about the countless absentees.

As well as work at the factory I would also continue to help my family at the clothing boutique Mile and Mira continued to promote.

Operating and running a store that has no customers had become a daily routine for many traders in the town, but the slightest hope of just one sale was enough to make it all worth while.

I remember one day in particular when I had offered to cover for one of the assistants who wanted time off.

As usual the store was empty of customers and I was counting the hours until it was time to leave. Unexpectedly, the door swung open and in stepped a black uniformed soldier, machinegun in hand. He swaggered towards me with an air of complete arrogance and I was shaken to the bone when I looked into his eyes. They were completely blank, holding no human emotion at all. Not wanting to show I was frightened by this oppressive barbarian figure, I stepped up politely and asked if he was looking for anything in particular. He beamed down at me, maybe a little surprised and told me he needed jeans. As I searched the racks for his size again the door swung open and there stood another black uniformed thug, machinegun hanging loosely at his side. This one was laughing uncontrollably and was obviously looking for fun or trouble. Hurriedly, I found the correct size and passed the jeans to the first man. I was shaking so much, but knew that to show fear could heighten their bravado and place me in even more danger than I already was.

Instead I asked, rather stupidly perhaps, if there was anything else he wanted. Sneering in my direction he snarled, "Yes, maybe there was something else here I would love dearly to try on for size!"

His crudeness only exasperated the others manic hysteria, but I stood politely in defiance without showing either fear or weakness.

They were unsure of themselves now and also of my own nationality as the boutique was in the 'right side of town'. Had this not have been the case, it is highly likely that the story would not have ended there and I would have suffered at their hands.

It is difficult to truly explain to those who have not experienced and suffered the true horrors of civil war. Like many towns and cities in Bosnia, Novi Travnik had been divided with unseen boundary lines. The right side of town simply meant you were amongst friends. Being on the wrong side of town however meant those around you were the enemy. A customary smile as the transaction was made could all too easily turn into attack and death. Luckily, on that day, my customers had come from the 'right side of town', had they come from the 'other side'; the story could have been quite different.

In those dark times, I also remember my little car. Andy, in his story remembers the sparrows and bacon rind. In my own story it is a car.

When I had finished college, I had begged and begged my father to buy me one. I was, after all, an adult now and needed transportation of my own, I would tell him.

In the end, his love for me gave way and he bought me a car. A Fico. Oh how I loved that car. It was the best present I had ever received, except possibly the little pull along toy dog Mom gave me when I was a girl. My little car brought so much fun and freedom. I recall having five people crammed into its tiny interior, everyone laughing and joking, having fun.

I awoke one morning and the car was gone. Her allotted space was empty and she was nowhere to be seen. I walked along the ravaged streets in the hope of finding her, but my little Fico had been stolen away from me as I slept.

Days later, I saw her. She was parked outside one of the cafés that had remained open despite the fighting. Sat drinking coffee outside, as if everything around them was normal, were the black uniformed militia who now controlled the town.

I hurried past my little car, so sad for my own loss, but even sadder knowing who now had her. They were sad figures in their own right, rifles and grenades in hand, bullying and beating anyone in their way, but how pathetic they still felt the need to take a little Fico to make them feel macho, big and clever.

War proves that nothing materialistic in our lives is important. I quickly found other things to care about other than my little car. I would pray over and over again the fighting would stop and life would resume some sense of normality. My prayers went unanswered however and the peace never came. Each day was to start as the previous had finished. Fear, misery and suffering would continue on unchanged as the sun rose and set each day.

\* \* \* \*

# Displaced

## Our Lives So Differently Told

# Chapter Twenty - Bratstvo – The End of the Dream

**I will never forget that fateful** day when I was truly exposed to the horrors of modern war.

Despite my inner loathing of the place, I was still working in the armaments factory where I felt it was my duty to scratch out a pittance; each dinar was now crucial if we were not to starve.

Every day, I was woken by my father telling me it was time to go to work. Oh how I had grown to hate those words. I would often wonder what the point was. Production was almost at a standstill and we were not even receiving our wages. Despite this, my parents were from a generation who found honour in punctuality and reliability and they would constantly point out that after the fighting, the factory would continue to operate and management would favour those who had remained loyal through the difficult times.

With this in mind, I always answered Dad's waking call, got up and dressed, ready for the day. Mom would have made breakfast, but I would not eat it. I felt sick and had pains in my stomach. All too soon, I would kiss them both goodbye at our front door and set out on the forty-five minute walk to work.

It was a beautiful August morning, the sun was shining and the birds were chirping their normal morning chorus, war was for a moment the last thing on my mind.

Once at the factory the day went on as usual. There was little work to do except going over some old blueprints and making some slight modifications to the machinery.

As lunchtime approached, the pains in my stomach were becoming unbearable and unable to stand the discomfort any longer, I decided to leave for home.

My workshop was on the far upper part of the factory next to the second exit. As I headed towards it, I suddenly heard a terrifyingly loud explosion and felt the ground shudder as if we had been hit by an earthquake.

Everyone around me froze as the whole building swayed as if it would fall to the ground at any moment. We looked at each other in shock and someone yelled,

"Everyone run, we are being bombed!"

I could not believe what was happening and felt I was caught up in some collective nightmare that was being shared by everyone around me.

Panic and mayhem began to take hold and I remember running and screaming so loud it felt like my lungs would burst from the sheer strain of my exertions. Over the screams and crashes as people and machinery collided, I could hear the terrifying sound of airplanes. Screeching so low and fast and followed quickly by the deafening sound of the bombs finding their targets and unleashing the horror for which they had been designed.

It was ironic. I stood within a building that's sole purpose had been to produce weapons of destruction. Now Bratstvo faced the wrath of her own creations like a mother facing off against her deadly offspring.

Blind with panic and deathly afraid, I cried for Mom. Just as I was about to abandon all hope of getting out of the factory alive, the strong arms of a fellow worker grabbed hold of me and pulled me along as we ran towards the exit, out the door and into his parked car. He told me to sit tight as he accelerated and weaved his frantic way through the rubble and debris that, only moments ago, had stood as a solid monument to the once great Yugoslavia.

To this day, I do not know who my saviour was, but I so hope he remained safe throughout the following years. Maybe one day our paths will cross again and I will be able to at long last tell him how much I appreciate the bravery which had almost definitely saved my life.

Similar scenes of horror met us as we raced into town. Four aircraft were screaming low over the buildings and discharging their deadly cargo in a hail of thunder and fire. The scene was more blockbuster movie than real life.

I kept asking myself how this could be happening; how could man show so much hatred for his brothers and sisters?

As we rounded a sharp corner, I came to my senses and asked to be let out of the car; I needed to find my family. He slammed on the breaks and I leapt from the vehicle and ran as fast as my aching and trembling legs could carry me.

I reached the family boutique, which, thankfully, had escaped intact. My friend was sheltering inside the store and told me she had not seen any of my family there.

More afraid than ever before, I dialled our home telephone number. Incredibly, it rang and Mom answered. She was crying and screaming so much that I could not understand anything she was saying.

I repeatedly begged her to calm down and listen to what I was saying. I told her I was safe and so too was my brother Mile.

I lied to my Mom. The last time I had seen Mile was as the bombs had started to fall on the factory, but I did not want to add to her panic. I quickly finished our conversation, assuring her that I would be home soon and then telephoned my sister. She too was crying hysterically and told me a bomb had exploded in front of her apartment and her husband was injured. With this news, the telephone line went dead.

Over my head, I could hear the airplanes approach yet again, the noise from their engines was deafening. I knew that I needed to get to my family and with this thought, I ran. True fear is indescribable and I would never want anyone to experience what I felt then. I knew this nightmare might be my last.

The streets were coated in debris and shattered glass and I passed the charred ruins caused by direct hits, but I kept running, even when my body told me it had suffered enough and wanted to give in. I was on autopilot, fuelled by adrenaline, desperate to reach the family apartment.

Finally, I burst through the front door and ran into the living room. Mom met me there and we held each other tight. Tears were streaming down her face in a mixture of shock, relief and despair.

I lied again that Mile was safe; that he had called into the boutique and I had spoken to him, all the while listening to my father stood on the balcony, hands outstretched and shouting to the planes overhead "How can you do this to the people? You are bombing the factory when you know that it is full of innocent people!"

Mom was horrified when I said that I was leaving the apartment to check on Mira. She begged me not to go back out onto the streets, but I ignored her pleas and once again ran from the building. I pushed my already exhausted body past limits I didn't even know it had until I found myself hurtling into the relative safety of Mira's apartment.

I was horrified to see her husband covered in blood. He was wearing a white jumpsuit which only exaggerated the terrible crimson stain spreading over him. In that one moment, I felt history was repeating itself. The recollection of my innocent Mom believing her own mother was asleep and covered in the crushed remnants of plums filled my mind and left me momentarily speechless.

Mira broke me from my spell, by telling me how these fresh injuries had occurred. Standing on the balcony, staring in disbelief at the scene unfolding before him, my brother-in-law had watched as the aircraft had flown in low over the buildings and shed their deadly cargo, narrowly missing the apartment complex and instead producing a huge crater below at least half the size of the whole four hundred unit building. Many innocent civilians had been saved by the near miss, but the full force of the backlash had hit the lone man staring out at the devastation.

What had happened on that day had been an inhumane act of cowardice, serving only to strengthen my resolve to make it through the nightmare. I was filled with the determination that, regardless of what was thrown at me and the people I loved and cared dearly about, I would continue on with the pride and dignity these monsters had tried so hard to strip away.

\* \* \* \*

# Displaced
## Our Lives So Differently Told

## Chapter Twenty One - Heading East

I lay awake that night reliving over and over again what I had seen and experienced throughout the day. The drone of the aircraft continued long after they had completed the job they had been sent to do and returned to base, never truly seeing the suffering and pain they had inflicted. Even now, years later, the sound of aircraft passing innocently overhead will ignite those awful memories and I find myself tumbling back in time to relive, once again, that terrifying August day.

Finally, this event had sparked a mass exodus of people from the town. I was soon to depart myself as I received an invitation from a friend to stay with him in Belgrade for as long as I wanted.

He had heard of the horrors that were spreading throughout Bosnia and said he would welcome both a friend and myself as his guests.

Within two days we were ready to leave and had secured tickets for the bus which would take us to the relative safety of Serbia. I later learnt that our bus had infact been the last one allowed to leave Novi Travnik and any person thereafter wishing to leave had to obtain permission to do so from the military authorities.

It was a terrible thing for me to do, leaving my family behind. Leaving loved ones is always difficult, but to leave them in the middle of a war zone is probably the hardest thing I have ever had to do in my whole life. The tears flowed as we hugged and kissed goodbye and I wondered, deep down, if I would ever see them again.

Standing, waiting for the bus to arrive, I prayed my family would be safe. Looking up into the clouds, I also wondered if God had any more surprises in store for me or if I were now to be left alone to live my life without the need for further suffering and distress.

With one final look back at the town I knew, I wished dearly I would never have to return and a safe new start was waiting for me in Belgrade.

As the bus slowly moved off, I withdrew deep into my own thoughts. I felt I was living the scenes of a blockbuster movie, still searching for the next instalment and the final plot twist.

In the modern world of DVD's and special features, all too often we are given the choice; to either take an active role in the movie experience or to simply be the audience. Do we sit and watch the true ending to the film, or the alternative? Rocky Balboa gave us the choice, we could sit and watch the age-old hero finally be defeated or, with the simple flick of a switch, we could watch him, with fondness, defeat the aggressor despite the overwhelming odds.

My own life at that time was like the tragic alternative. I now hoped for the other, happier ending where I finally got to belong.

The bus weaved its way through the once beautiful landscape of Bosnia. My initial relief turned to dread as I saw the carnage all around me. Wherever I looked, houses had been destroyed and whole villages were deserted and left abandoned as if some mystical force had simply removed everything living and left the rest to burn and rot. Burnt out vehicles littered the road and the bus driver struggled to keep us moving through the hell which had descended all around.

The horrors of the first air strikes against Novi Travnik seemed trivial to what was unfurling in front of us with the passing of each mile. This was destruction and human madness at its very worst. If hell was a living entity, then here it was for all to witness its testimony and vile agony.

As my brain began to numb itself to the fresh horrors each corner of the road offered my gaze, I wondered deeply how such a thing could happen. How the rest of the world could sit and watch in the comfort of easy chairs and surround sound television, whilst the people of Bosnia were succumbing to madness and slaughter.

Again my thoughts turned to Grandfather's lost brother in England. Was it possible that he still lived to watch the carnage repeated in the country of his birth and if not, was there still a deep enough connection there that thought was being given to the pain and suffering being felt by the people left behind?

Slowly, as we trudged on, the fires subsided and the border drew near. We were finally leaving the glowing embers of a ruined Bosnia behind, with great relief to everyone on board.

The bus driver was signalled to pull over at the military checkpoint. Formidable, expressionless border control personnel entered the bus and closely scrutinized everyone aboard. Luggage was emptied and every item was inspected individually.

Men were led off the bus to undergo a more in-depth examination and line of questioning until finally the bus was given the all clear and we were allowed to continue, crossing the invisible line that meant safety and Serbia.

Once across the border, we vacated the bus and made our way to the town house we would be guests in.

The family welcomed us with open arms and made us comfortable in their home. We stayed with the family there for two days before travelling south to the second house they owned and used for vacations.

Everything seemed just too good to be true and I remember pinching my arm to make sure I was not experiencing some idyllic dream and would awake once again to the sound of aeroplanes and exploding bombs.

The neighbours were an old couple and welcomed us each morning with something freshly cooked for breakfast. I felt the pangs of guilt that here I was, safe and in beautiful surroundings, whilst those I loved were trapped in the bloodshed sweeping across Bosnia.

On the fourth day we were startled from sleep with heavy hammering on the door. Once opened, I was shocked to see three men, all with long hair and beards. They had the same look in their eyes I had first seen in the faces of the black uniformed thugs in my hometown and this sent a shiver down my spine.

One of the men put his foot in the doorway and asked coldly,

"Are you Serbs, Orthodox?"

"Does it matter?" I stupidly answered.

The men were obviously shocked at my response and their aggression manifested itself in their expressions instantly. Quickly I blurted out,

"Yes of course we are Serbian and of the Orthodox religion."

This eased the tension immediately and an eerie smile spread across their faces in unison. The one who had spoken told us tonight they would take us out and we must be ready when they returned later.

I realised in that instant we had not simply been asked out on a date, our invitation to join them had in fact been an order which had to be obeyed or there would be consequences.

Nervously during the afternoon, we got ourselves ready for the uncertainty that was to follow in the evening. We were so frightened and when at 6pm the same knock hammered the front door, we froze.

The three bearded men were there and dressed this time in some kind of crude military uniform. They beckoned us in to their waiting car and drove into the small town, to a bar that was blasting out ear deafening music.

As we sat at the nearest available table, I noticed with sheer horror each one of the men was armed and had grenades hanging from their belts.

I knew we were in the gravest of danger. We should do nothing to upset our 'dates' and above all else, we had to pretend we were enjoying their company and that we were there by choice, rather than because we had been ordered there.

Fear is a difficult emotion to handle, regardless of how many times you experience it.

I found, however, fear can be overcome, especially when your very survival is in the balance. I agreed with everything they said, smiled and played the part in order to make them feel as though I was honoured to be in their company.

With agonising cruelty the evening wore on, until finally the leader of the three bellowed out that he was 'sick of this stupid place' and ordered everyone to leave.

I knew from the madness glistening in his eyes that something terrible was about to happen. Like frightened schoolchildren waiting to be punished, we followed them outside to the car.

Before climbing inside, the same man slowly unclipped a grenade from his waist and threw it into the entrance of the bar. With breakneck speed, he leapt into the car and with wheels screeching, we careered wildly away from the thunderous explosion which followed.

They were laughing hysterically, fuelled by the potent drugs: insanity and evil. Fear began pulsing through me and I fought desperately to keep it at bay. These men were capable of murder and had just proved they had no limits and little conscience. I knew the killing of two innocent women was well within their grasp.

For what seemed like an eternity, the car was driven through the streets as if in a race, until finally it came to a stop outside a house. We were ushered out of the car and into the gloomy interior of the dilapidated building.

I remember whispering to my friend to agree with anything the men wanted and our lives now depended on how we reacted to the situation before us.

We were told to sit and accepted the drink offered with trembling hands.

With menace and scorn in his voice, the leader leant over and asked if we were from Bosnia and if we were Muslim. I again stated we were of the Orthodox faith and the people of Bosnia are varied and follow many faiths, not just the Islamic one.

The whole night was full of sickening questions and veiled threats and I knew I must remain sober and coherent if we were to survive the night.

Maybe the gods were looking down at us that night, as with the rising sun we were allowed to leave.

We walked home in silence and once there tumbled into bed. I slept the whole day as if my body was shielding itself from the night's events.

The following afternoon, I telephoned Mom to make sure my family there were safe. Maybe she recognised the fear in my voice, or maybe it was the close connection that unites a mother and daughter, but she knew something bad had happened to me and urged me to at least think about returning home.

With deep sadness, I realised that the safety of Serbia had been nothing more than a dream.

I also knew our ordeal that night would not be an isolated incident and the three men would return. We had escaped with our lives, but I knew next time we might not be so lucky. We were totally helpless in the hands of crazed thugs who answered to no one.

With heavy hearts and fear of the unknown weighing us down, we decided to return to Bosnia. We would face whatever demons lay there.

We headed north to Belgrade and gave the family there our grateful thanks as we handed back the keys to the house that should have been our shelter.

Next day, we got back on a bus to take us over the border into the madness our country had become.

The slow drive towards Bosnia was impeded every couple of miles by military check points. The bus and its occupants would be thoroughly searched for weapons or anything else that could aid the rising levels of violence and bloodshed smothering the land in front of us.

The road was littered with military vehicles in a morbid show of firepower and strength.

Once across the border things worsened. Again, the bus was constantly stopped and searched, however this time they were not regular soldiers, but more like extras from some unrealistic war movie. They wore bandanas and masks as if competing to see who could instil the most fear into the civilians.

The bus rumbled on regardless, until I was awoken from slumber by panicked cries from the front of the bus. Straining to see what was happening, I first saw that we had once again been stopped at a checkpoint. Then I realised we were in a far graver situation then which we had already faced along the road.

This point was manned by the infamous Bosnian elite paramilitary. They were notorious and feared for their complete and utter disrespect for human life and the stories of their atrocities were countless. Torture, rape, murder and mutilation had become a seemingly everyday pastime to the men now standing between us and our continued survival.

In that instant I feared we would never see the other side of the checkpoint and began to ready myself for the worst. Amazingly, I was startled from my thoughts by the sound of laughter. I looked up in disbelief and saw that some of the militia were laughing and shaking the hands of one of the other passengers. Immediately, I recognised her as the wife of a well-known comedian from the town of Travnik.

Her famous husband had been waiting at the checkpoint for her. In the excitement of being faced with such a high profile figure, the militia men opened up the checkpoint and waved the bus through to continue its journey.

Fatigue finally claimed my body and the rest of the journey passed in the blink of an eye.

I somehow arrived at my parent's apartment and remember the tears of joy as Mom held me tightly in the safety of her bosom, as if she was holding a crying little girl that bruised her knees falling in the street.

Finally the hugs and tears of our reunited family subsided. After a hastily cooked supper, I withdrew to the comfort of the familiar bed that I had left behind in the hope of a better life across the border.

Next morning, Mom spoke about the possibility of me travelling to the safety of Croatia. She explained one of our neighbours had moved there before the hostilities had begun and had settled in the coastal town of Split.

I did not want to leave my family again and told Mom I would hear not of it. My place was now here with the family I loved, regardless of the perilous situation we were in.

Later that day I visited my sister. Mira explained in order for the family to survive we needed money to buy essential items were now rocketing in price and becoming hard to get hold of. Everyone in Bosnia was out of work and no jobs could be found in the country. Mira told me the only way forward now was to leave for Croatia.

\* \* \* \*

# Displaced

## Our Lives So Differently Told

## Chapter Twenty Two - Heading West

**Still with great reluctance, I eventually** succumbed to the family's persistent advice. Leaving was the only option and I was once again to abandon my hometown and attempt to tap into the clothing market in Croatia. After all, why try and sell fashionable garments in a town where people could not even afford to buy the basic necessities.

Within days I had arrived in Split. With great kindness, our old neighbour offered me a place with him and his family in their apartment.

Jure was a great guy and I loved him dearly, but oh how he could talk and talk without stopping, even to breath! Day after day, I would have to endure the constant drone of stories and gossip. I often wondered how Jure's wife and children could stand to hear them repeated every single day.

I relayed to my sister that I could not tolerate the constant bombardment and so Mira recommended including Jure in our enterprise. She thought if he were kept busy then he would have less time to constantly talk.

Unfortunately, Mira was wrong. His never-ending stories were no longer confined to the apartment. Now, I would also have to face the barrage whilst I struggled to establish the family business in this strange place.

Obviously, I didn't know my way around this new town and so Jure finally became a help instead of a hindrance, although he could not tell his left from his right and so would direct me around the streets using his watch, which he always wore on his left wrist.

One day however, he forgot his watch. Pandemonium reigned supreme and we rarely found ourselves at the places we had intended to visit that day. Trade was slow to say the least.

Even whilst we were conducting business with prospective customers, Jure would speak non-stop. Often, the customer would become so distracted they would forgot why they had been interested in the first place and we would leave empty handed with nothing to show for our efforts.

One-day things finally came to a head and I asked him simply not to speak at all and instead let me continue carrying out the day's transactions in peace.

I remember Jure replying that in all honesty he could not remain silent and he had an uncontrollable urge to talk. He simply had a deep-rooted desire to hear his own voice, constantly.

From that day on I decided the only way I would be able to scratch a living was to go it alone. Croatia was not the gold paved land my family had believed and the same economic problems facing them back in Bosnia had made their way here too.

Without Jure's directions I struggled to find my way through the streets of Split, although I did revel in my newly acquired silence.

One day, whilst hopelessly lost, a Police car stopped me. The officer walked in circles around my car and began laughing. The sound disturbed and frightened me so I asked why I had been stopped. The officer simply looked at me and told me he had recognised the cars registration plate. Not only was it a Bosnian registration, but also from the same area he had once lived.

I was so relieved and, after chatting for a while, agreed that he could take me out to one of the bars in town.

Maybe I made a mistake agreeing to that drink. As the weeks wore on, he became a little obsessed with me and would call in to see me daily. His invitations to take me out turned into what seemed like orders and I didn't feel as if I could say no. I became increasingly worried for my safety if I ever refused him.

Eventually I relayed my fears to my sister and expressed my desire to return home. Mira would have none of this, however and announced she would travel to stay with me for a short while in Croatia instead.

I was so relieved when Mira arrived. Jure and his family had been so kind and I will always be grateful to them, but I had felt so alone in Split without my family and friends.

Mira and I spent the next few cold wintry days trying desperately to sell clothing, but found that we were fighting a losing battle.

Prospective customers would pick up on our Bosnian accents and simply retract from the sale. With dignity, we held our heads high, but inside we knew the hard truth. We were thought of almost as lepers and the healthy people around us feared they too would be infected if they associated themselves with us.

After spending six days with me in Split, Mira had to return home to her family. With great sadness, she packed up her belongings whilst I sat watching television, the prospect of being alone once again hanging heavily on my shoulders.

Suddenly, news bulletins interrupted the scheduled programming to tell of the spiralling conflict between the Croatians and Muslims; aggression between the two was spreading.

Television reports indicated Bosnia was a no go area and the majority of the roads were blocked by military units or local militia. We sat together in silence, but our thoughts were the same. The family we had left behind were now in even greater peril and there was nothing we could do to help them. They were isolated, on their own in the grip of hell's jaws.

Once again, historical hatred and cultural division were rising like bile from the depths of Bosnia's belly. Now the crazed would rule, leaving the innocents to suffer in a way not seen since 1945.

Hours turned into days with nothing in the way of contact. Finally I remember Jure's neighbour coming to the apartment to tell us that my brother was on the telephone and wanted to speak to us urgently.

Fearing something was terribly wrong, I ran up the stairs to speak with him. Mile was on the line and I knew instantly this was not a social call.

I remember feeling the whole world stood still as he gave me the news. Father had died.

It was not the war that had killed him though; he had suffered a heart attack.

I remember the numbness that crept over my entire body and left me unable to move from that spot. I felt like a frightened child.

By the time I was able to compose myself and walk downstairs, I was shaking and crying so much it was difficult to see. Mira instantly knew something terrible had happened and rushed to me, embracing me like she always did when I was upset. She held me so tight and I finally had the strength to blurt out the news. We stood holding each other for what seemed like an eternity, united in grief.

We knew we had to return home straight away, regardless of the conflict sweeping across the country.

All morning we spent at the bus depot asking every driver we came across if they were heading into Bosnia. The answer was the same; Bosnia was a no go area and now only the insane would try and make the journey.

Just as we were losing all hope of getting home to see Father one last time, a man in uniform came to us and asked us if we needed transport into central Bosnia. After explaining that we needed to get there as soon as possible, he pointed to a nearby bus and told us we were free to travel with him and his colleagues. Relieved, we boarded and as we did I noticed that all the other passengers were soldiers. We were the only civilians onboard.

This added to the heightened fear of what we might find as we entered Bosnia. Given my previous experiences, my mind ran wild with all kinds of horrors that could be lurking across the border.

I was invited to sit next to one of the soldiers at the rear of the bus. Once we started our journey, the soldier broke the silence and began asking me questions. The innocent conversation soon turned into what seemed to be more like an interrogation.

I felt history was being repeated and the same fear I had felt whilst in the company of the militiamen in Serbia washed over me. I knew if the truth came out that we were orthodox in faith, then we would be in grave danger. Instead of telling him the truth and fuelling his rising suspicions, I gave him the details of a Croatian friend and his family. Despite this, his constant interruptions, never ending questions and cynical laugh made me dread what was coming.

Once across the border, the bus stopped at the roadside. Suspecting something was wrong, I asked my interrogator what was happening. He replied that the bus would now have to stop every few miles in order for the road ahead to be made safe and cleared of ambush and snipers.

He explained the journey that should have taken five hours to complete could now take two days, depending on the road and how fierce the fighting was.

From the relative safety of Split, we had unwittingly made ourselves a target for snipers, artillery fire and ambush. Each and every noise would chill me. Not a minute passed by without my imagining I was in the cross hairs of a sniper's rifle, finger paused on the trigger, careful not to waste his shot.

After hours of this, extreme fatigue took hold and I drifted into an uneasy sleep. I eventually awoke to the feel of warming sunshine on my face. No sooner had I opened my eyes then the questions resumed.

Although we had been travelling for most of the day and throughout the night, we were still a long way from Novi Travnik. The realisation sank in that despite enduring this journey, we would not make it in time for Father's burial.

My body and mind were fast approaching breaking point and I only vaguely remember the rest of the hellish two-day journey.

I had missed the funeral of my own father and this weighed heavily on my conscience. The father who had raised and cared for me so very much and I had not been there to say a final farewell.

I remember stepping off the bus and into a smothering darkness. I was drawn back into reality with the ice-cold shock of snow being packed around my neck to rouse me from unconsciousness. My body had reached its limit and my brain had simply turned out the lights.

We quickly learnt things were now very different in Novi Travnik. Fierce fighting was widespread and the town was divided into two parts. My parents had been forced to move, their apartment had simply been on the wrong side of town and where they now lived was virtually impossible to either get into or out of.

In desperation, we headed for the family boutique in the hope someone would be there. Luckily one of the assistants was and gave us directions to the apartment Mom now lived in.

We carefully made our way through the streets and even from outside the building, I could hear the grief stricken cries that were instantly recognisable as coming from my mother.

We raced inside the apartment and embraced her without the need for words. I felt pangs of guilt hit me at the thought of not being here when Mom had needed me the most.

As the initial shock of grief gradually began to subside, we learnt fighting had erupted one night and my parents had been forced to flee their apartment and dodge heavy gunfire and grenade attacks.

As the days passed, the fighting intensified and Father began to suffer under the stress and strain of the conflict. One morning, he had called at the boutique and complained of a pain in his chest. On arriving back at the apartment, the pain had intensified and he had rung the doorbell in the hope someone inside would come to his aid.

Sadly, before anyone reached the door, he had succumbed to a massive heart attack and could not be revived.

The days and weeks that followed saw me slide into the depths of despair. My resilience and spirit were all but broken and I had become a mere shadow of the happy, hippy girl from my academy days in Zagreb.

I refused to venture outside despite the constant encouragement from Mira and confined myself indoors, finding safety and comfort in Mom's company.

Eventually though, the blackness and utter misery which had crept and crawled deep inside of me, subsided. I realised that in order to survive I would have to rise above the situation and live as normal an existence as was possible in the middle of the carnage and death surrounding me.

With apprehension, I made the first step and slowly opened the door of the apartment. I remember being awed at the colours and light that I had withdrawn myself from for so long.

Spring was in full swing and, despite the fact I was in the middle of a bloody and desperate war zone, I was taken aback by just how beautiful the very basics of human existence were. I marvelled at the dappled sunshine and sheer wonder of nature. I could feel the healing process starting in my mind and body.

With my newly found inner strength and determination, I decided to walk into town and visit the family boutique. I became more and more horrified at the scene unfolding before me.

Buildings I had known had simply disappeared, to be replaced with piles of debris. Almost every place that remained standing was deeply scarred, windows were shattered and sickening large holes adorned the walls. I remember thinking god had offered us heaven, but here in Novi Travnik we had chosen hell.

Once at the boutique, I was told Mira had left to get coffee at one of the few shops still trading, so I hurried through the rubble-filled streets and had a moment of shock at how quiet the coffee shop was. I remembered this being a busy, bustling centre for the local gossips. Now it was almost deserted, with no more than ten people sitting in silence, lost in their own thoughts.

Both Mila and Mira were there taking coffee and were surprised and relieved to see that I had finally broken free of my self-imposed incarceration.

Foolishly, I asked Mile where were all the people that would normally be in here, exchanging gossip and catching up on the news of the day. As usual he was quick in his response and asked me if I thought I was still miles away in the comfort and safety of Split. He went on to say those who remained amongst the rubble and despair of Novi Travnik were those that were trapped here and had nowhere else to go. The conflict had escalated into a full blown war whilst I had locked myself away and we must hope and pray that peace came quickly before it was too late.

Over the next few days, I became a regular customer to the isolated coffee shop. The communal sharing of the horror stories became a sort of comfort to me as we were there living it collectively and not alone.

It was during one of my visits to the shop, affectionately known as Tomato, that I met my future husband, Tonci, for the very first time. He was so different from the other men who gathered there. He seemed so calm and gentle and didn't idle away the moments relaying the horrors of war. He would speak as if we were simply taking coffee on his lunch break, enjoying each others company away from the rigours of work.

He was the breath of fresh air I became instantly attracted to and I would find myself seeking out his company whenever I was away from the confines of the apartment or boutique.

Mira, as sisters do, recognised the spring in my step which had been missing for so long. She immediately asked who it was who lifted my spirits so high. I confided that I had begun to fall for Tonci's charm and found myself drawn to him whenever he was near.

Later that afternoon we were walking and I noticed Tonci was ahead of us with a group of his friends. Shyly, I asked Mira if we could rest a while on the bench a little further along the street from where the men stood.

Like a little girl, lost in a fairytale, I gazed down at the ground, not wanting to catch his gaze, whilst Mira and I spoke.

Finally daring myself to look upwards, I found his gaze fixed firmly on my own. For what seemed like an age, our eyes remained locked together in mutual attraction and curiosity.

My heart thundered like a run away train as Tonci rose from his resting place and without taking his eyes off mine, walked purposefully across the pavement towards our bench and politely asked if he could join us.

Mira gestured a welcome whilst I simply sat there like a wild animal frozen in the oncoming beams of a car.

Whilst he spoke, I realised I was falling in love and knew I was helpless to stop, or even slow, the tide of emotions washing over me.

Over the following days and weeks, my thoughts were filled only with Tonci. Like most men, he had been drafted into one of the military units formed to defend the town. Every time it was his turn to stand on the front line, I would become restless. Deep down I knew, whatever time we spent together might be the last. My one moment of happiness amidst the fear and torture could be cruelly snatched away from me at any time.

When we are deeply in love, the people closest to us can feel it and it was not long before Mom asked who it was that had stolen her baby's heart.

I simply could not contain the words pouring out of me and told her all about Tonci. The words came thick and fast and I remember Mom telling me to slow down and take a breath.

I told her I had a boyfriend I cared for so much and we had been spending as much time together as was possible in these troubled times.

Surprisingly, Mom let down the defences she had always placed around me and seemed to instantly warm to the man I described.

She had always treated my previous boyfriends with suspicion and mistrust. They had been the easy-going, carefree hippy guys from my days in Zagreb. Now it was a huge surprise that she wanted to meet Tonci. She told me to invite him to the apartment as soon as possible.

"If he makes my baby happy, then I am happy" she told me.

* * * *

# Displaced

## Our Lives So Differently Told

## Chapter Twenty Three - Love Amidst the Fear

**The afternoon was a dream, a stark reversal** of the daily nightmare Novi Travnik had become.

Tonci came to the apartment and was welcomed with open arms by Mom. She connected with him, like I had done, instantly. She disclosed that although never knowing anything of Tonci himself, she had known his father, who had been a bus driver in the town.

The afternoon flowed effortlessly in the company I loved and cherished. We had refreshing conversation and I felt a deep happiness flow through me.

Mom happily welcomed Tonci into the family.

I look back now and see that she had not shown such happiness since Dad had died. The glint in her eye and her warm smile had finally returned.

Mom's blessing was crucial to me and I remember crying myself to sleep that night as I replayed her words to me; he was a nice man worthy of her precious daughter.

As love was blossoming between us, the violence and bloodshed was escalating.

The enemy's stranglehold on Novi Travnik tightened and the town became embroiled in a bitter struggle for survival. During the daylight hours, sirens would sound relentlessly to warn of incoming mortar and artillery fire. It seemed nothing was to be spared from the destruction and deadly projectiles would be fired indiscriminately at both military and civilian targets. In the darkness of the night, it would be the snipers readying themselves for their misguided moment of glory. Scanning through magnifying lenses, they would pick out anything daring to move through the deserted streets. Then there was the music. The enemy had installed loud speakers on the mountains surrounding the town and would play their music throughout the night to deprive us of our sleep, torturing us further.

Before long, the bass line of some unknown song fired at us with the precision of the gunfire that accompanied it. In the blackout interior of the apartment, it became difficult to distinguish night from day.

Only the rare sight of a moonless sky would entice the condemned out of their homes to forage for food and water. We were now entombed in the living hell of what Bosnian life had become.

Each day the men of the town would be summoned to where the weapons were stored and ordered to take their allotted rifle. Ammunition was becoming scarce and uniforms were almost non existent. All men of fighting age, regardless of status, were now expected to fight and defend the town. Farmer, bar owner and the simple woodcutter were now forced to take up the instruments of death. The choice, however, was a simple one now. Kill the enemy or allow the enemy to kill us.

Once armed, the men would be ordered to their positions on the front line. The bedraggled procession was the same each and every day. Untrained combatants, most without even recognisable uniform, were simply ordered to stand and defend against the aggressors before them.

Months of fierce, unrelenting fighting had taken a heavy toll. The men were tired, physically and emotionally.

It was now commonplace for some of the men to break under the strain. They attempted to find a place to escape from the horror by taking refuge in basements of derelict buildings or apartments roofs where they would be exposed to the sharp eyes of the waiting snipers. They would even risk death by hiding in their own freezer chests; now empty of food, they were big enough to hide a man.

Units were formed to find the absent men that had not collected their weapons. Once found they would be sent to the zones exposed to the heaviest fighting. In most cases this was almost certainly a death sentence.

I remember the look of utter abandonment which could be seen on the faces of everyone. It felt like the world had turned its back on the people of Bosnia, leaving us to suffer in silence.

No longer did we see the welcoming respite the convoys of United Nations personnel offered. No longer were we offered the much needed supplies of food and water from the world's aid agencies. We were now so very alone; we had no food or water. Electricity had become a distant luxurious memory and our movements were heavily restricted in an attempt to keep ourselves out of the crosshairs.

At times it felt like we were living out a grotesque circus performance, only here the reward for performing was not applause from the watching audience, but a minutes respite from the death that stalked us.

Each morning the topic of conversation would be the same; who had succumbed in the night to the barbarity of our attackers? Had it been mortar fire? The work of a sniper? Or had the victims been caught trying to escape, executed and sent back into town for all to see.

Whatever the reasons for their sad demise, the dead would be stored in the basements of the broken apartments and garages until it was safe to bury them under a moonless sky.

I recall in particular, the unimaginable grief of a mother who learnt a third son had died. To lose one son would be hard enough for any woman who had carried and raised a child. To lose three would drive anyone into the perilous depths of despair.

Despite it all, Tonci and I decided to get married. We had initially planned to wait for the fighting to stop and had hoped the ceremony would take place outside. However, we had heard that one last convoy was to be allowed out of the siege and young, married couples were to be given the first option to leave.

Hastily over the coming weeks, we arranged our special day with the meagre scraps that could be foraged. We managed to obtain a litre of Slivovitz costing us $100, one pack of cigarettes and two pounds of horsemeat, which had been given to us as a wedding present.

On November 5$^{th}$, the simple service took place in Mom's apartment. Mom and Mira were the witnesses and my brother Mile, his wife and a friend who had brought a guitar, were the only people that could be packed into the tiny room. As we said our vows in the darkness, the serenade was not that of bells and organ music, but gunfire.

After a little singing to the strummed chords of my friend's guitar, it was time to say our farewells and leave for Tonci's apartment. This was the custom following marriage; a custom Tonci's mother insisted we kept despite the dangers of what awaited anyone foolish enough to step outside.

We ran in silence through the deserted streets in fear we would be picked off by a sniper. The war was raging on despite our happy day.

Once inside the apartment I was horrified at the sight that met me. The walls were riddled with bullet holes.

The building stood on the very front line and was constantly targeted by the enemy.

Next morning, Tonci explained that at times the militia would be as close as fifty metres from the apartment and would fire blindly into the windows in the hope of claiming another faceless kill.

Both Tonci and Mile would be drafted daily to the front line, yet Mile refused to carry a weapon. He said maintained he could not and would not kill another human being.

Instead he went to war armed with an umbrella. Each day he would wake, get dressed and leave the apartment carrying it as if it were a rifle. Maybe it would have been a benefit to him in the rain, but served no protection against open warfare.

Tonci was drafted into the part of town where fighting was at its fiercest. He told us on his return in that area of town, people had been trapped in their apartments for six months. The only water they had was from whatever seeped through the walls in the basement and they had become so hungry they had been forced to eat the plants they had once kept as decoration.

As the siege continued, the inhabitable places were becoming scarce; most buildings now had been reduced to rubble. Mile, his wife Duska and their two young sons Vanja and Saša moved into the apartment with Mom, Tonci and I.

For safety against the constant shrapnel which whistled through the air we placed two chest freezers, covered in cloth, against the window. Even during the daylight hours, we were now starved of sunlight and we were hemmed in the apartment's dank interior, bumping into each other as we moved around the cramped space.

Mom would busy herself making meals out of practically nothing. She always amazed me with what she managed to produce to keep us fed.

One day in particular, she was preparing the days dish when a grenade landed in front of our building. Pieces of shrapnel escaped the shield of the freezers and screeched through the room, narrowly missing her head. She was so angry, not that we had been targeted, but the attack had come at an inconvenient time and ruined the food she was preparing.

Throughout those months of despair and anguish, Mom remained a pillar of strength to us all. She would fill the long, dark days and nights with endless stories from World War II and the survival tips she had learnt as a child.

She showed us how we could improvise candles using a glass of water with a little oil poured onto the surface and then a cotton thread could be lit as the wick.

Mom was the person to carry me through the darkest days of my life. Without her support, guidance and comfort, my own story would have been so very different.

\* \* \* \*

# Displaced

## Our Lives So Differently Told

## Chapter Twenty Four - Women and War

**Western eyes had labelled our fate,** 'Ethnic Cleansing'. Their idea of cleansing was our idea of murder. My new husband Tonci and brother Mile had been press ganged to join the armed struggle to defend our town and its people, but women had a different role to play in the war. We were to suffer the same hardships and dangers as the men, but we were also to carry the burden of worrying for our loved ones stood on the front line.

Whilst the men of the household were out fighting, it was left to the womenfolk to carry out the daily rituals of cooking, washing and cleaning. Food was becoming increasingly scarce and we would find ourselves rummaging through other peoples garbage for any scraps they had unwittingly thrown away. Rubbish accumulated everywhere with no one brave, or stupid, enough to risk depositing it outside.

The stench in the apartments became intolerable. Food decay, lack of sanitation, sweat and the smell of death filled the air and there was no escape. Coffins were rested amongst the piles of garbage in the corridors. Only in the relative safety of the night could the dead be laid to rest, hastily buried wherever a vacant plot of land could be found.

Flies revelled in their new found paradise and came in swarms to feast on the debris of war. Each apartment was literally crawling with the winged invaders. Even sleep could not offer respite. Like vultures circling a corpse, the flies would constantly land and crawl across us, checking to see if we had yet succumbed.

Even worse was to come. Many households had kept dogs as family pets before the war, but now, unable to feed themselves never mind their animals, many families abandoned them to fend for themselves. Hunger, fear and suffering quickly reversed evolution and the dogs turned feral, more wolf than man's best friend.

Naturally a pack animal, the dogs roamed the streets in numbers seeking anything edible. In the shadow of the moon, the patient sniper was no longer the only one searching out movement along the derelict streets. Now there was also a bloodthirsty pack of dogs to avoid. Fierce hunger had driven them to attack whenever the opportunity presented itself. Only when it was completely necessary would a bullet be used to ward off an attack. Ammunition was scarce and couldn't be wasted, however humane such an end would be.

Foraging for water could only take place at night when clouds blanketed the moon and the stars. You cannot truly realise how much water you need just to survive until there comes a time when you have none.

We would wash the laundry in plastic containers so the dirty water could be reused for the toilets. They had to be emptied by hand due to the sewers being blocked, either by explosion or sabotage.

Every drop of water that we used had to be found outside and manually brought in. We would search blindly in the darkness and then hurriedly carry containers through the streets.

Occasionally, the waiting snipers would fire blindly into the darkness in the hope of hitting an unseen target. They knew we would be outside gathering water and the lightening streaks of tracer fire would whistle overhead. The feeling of waiting for that impact, waiting for a bullet to slash skin and bone, will forever stay with me. Each retort of some distant, unseen rifle froze your very soul. Only when the tracer screeched past would you dare to take in your next breath.

As if foraging for water was not bad enough, we would also have to gather firewood. Winters in Novi Travnik could be extreme and bitterly cold so in order to survive, we had to heat the apartment constantly. Wood was also needed for cooking as electricity supplies had been cut months previously.

Collecting wood was far more dangerous than foraging for water as this had to be done during the daytime. As the supplies of wood dwindled from the ruined bombed-out buildings, we were forced further from the cover of town and onto the surrounding hills occupied by the enemy.

As we hurriedly chopped down the trees before marauding patrols could reach us, they would fire their rifles from their positions and we would run, zig-zag fashion, in a desperate attempt to avoid becoming another statistic.

Once cut, we would load the timber onto a large wooden wheelbarrow that Dad had made and run as fast as we could back to the apartment with our prize.

I remember one day in particular when we had risked our lives chopping and collecting firewood. We were hurrying back down the hillside towards town with our wheelbarrow laden with chopped timber when we were startled by the loud blare of a car horn behind us. I lost control of the barrow and the precious cargo cascaded to the ground.

The car skidded to a stop by our side and the occupants got out, laughing and pointing at our plight. They mocked and told us that they were glad we had turned into animals, forced to forage in the woods for scraps of food and water.

I struggled to keep my anger at bay, but realised any retaliation would result in death. They ordered us to leave the wood where it had fallen and run down the hill empty handed, back to the hellhole that awaited us there.

Evenings were spent confined in the cramped apartment. In the darkness nothing could be done and conversation became a new pastime. Mom would reminisce about her youth and recall with fondness the exploits of her father and his brother, Maksim. Somehow the brothers had captured an enemy radio and would trick the them into dispatching air support claiming they were allies to the occupying forces and under heavy attack.

Adrenaline fuelled fighter pilots would appear over the mountain tops and unwittingly attack their own forces in the carpeted forest below.

She recalled Maksim leaving suddenly to take the fight deeper into Bosnia.

Despite being at war, the villagers had to continue with their daily work to support their families through those darkest of times.

Men and women would tend the crops and livestock as if nothing else mattered. Occasionally however, the tolling of the church bell resounded down along the valleys. Calling the flock, not to god, but to take up arms against an encroaching threat to the village. The bells of peace had been turned against everything they stood for and were openly used to signal a call to arms. Once the threat had been removed, weapons were hidden and again the mountain slopes were littered with people going about their daily routines.

Like in all wars, men dominated the fighting role in the remote villages of Bosnia. They were the soldiers, the strategists and overall commanders. Women were the ones keeping families together and ensuring day-to-day survival. The bullet and grenade cared nothing of gender and women were targeted as equals, constantly straying into sniper fire to ensure meagre rations of food and water were collected and prepared to nourish their loved ones. Man had the trigger, but it was woman who kept the very fabric of humanity alive at home.

\* \* \* \*

# Displaced

## Our Lives So Differently Told

## Chapter Twenty Five - Hope at Last

**The desperate living conditions were taking** their own toll on the condemned inhabitants of the town.

I recall with horror the day that I was combing my hair and heard something fall out onto the chair. I was mortified to see a tiny crawling louse. My screams brought Tonci and Mile rushing into the room. How they laughed at my sad plight. The more they laughed, the more I cried.

"How can this be?" I screamed, tugging at my hair. I had been dragged down so low that now my body was infested with dirty lice.

Luckily and due to the fact it was not edible, anti-louse lotion was widely available and I quickly rid my head of the scurrying invaders.

Head lice were a common feature of the siege and it had become a perfectly normal sight to see children with their heads shaved to ward off the unwelcome visitors.

Typhoid also became a common threat amongst the living and everyone awaited its inevitable arrival as winter gave way to the warmer climates of spring and summer. Non-existent sanitation spread the deadly germs that lurked in the rotting faeces and most villagers would succumb to stomach upsets and pain.

One morning I was asked by Mira to meet her at the improvised coffee bar which had been erected in the shelter of bombed out buildings. There was obvious panic in her voice and I feared the worst. On the way, I called at the makeshift market and bought two cigarettes for ten deutsche marks (eggs were seven deutsche marks each, a jar of home made jam would set you back thirty).

On reaching the coffee bar I found Mira huddled at one of the tables in tears. She explained that during the previous night, military police wearing masks to conceal their identity had knocked on the door to her apartment. Fearing she was about to be robbed, Mira had first run to where the money from the boutique had been stored, hid it in her underwear and then opened the door.

Once inside the apartment, the masked visitors demanded to know the whereabouts of Darko, Mira's husband. She explained he was away, working for the United Nations as an interpreter.

They demanded to know his exact whereabouts as he had failed to turn up for military service. Again, Mira explained he had been asked to act as interpreter to the peacekeeping forces of the UN.

The masked intruders finally accepted what Mira had told them and turned their attention to theft. They demanded she hand over any money she had in the apartment. To exaggerate their menace, one of them pulled her towards him and brutally placed the barrel of his weapon under her chin.

She had suspected when she allowed them access into the apartment that the visit would turn into a robbery, so had left a small amount of cash unhidden. Disgruntled that they had neither found her husband nor come across a substantial amount of money, they left, smashing furniture and breaking everything in their path to the door.

Just as it seemed things could never return to normality, Novi Travnik and its people were about to be freed from the living hell that had not only consumed them, but the whole of Bosnia. The West had decided enough was enough. Bloody war on their doorstep was no longer acceptable, despite the bloodshed being in its fourth year now.

International pressure and military intervention had forced the opposing factions into debate around the table and not aggression on the battlefield.

I will never forget the day I sat waiting for Tonci to return from the front line of that dirty war. He had an unusual spring in his step as he approached and I asked him what was wrong. Without saying anything in reply, he produced chocolate from his pocket and his whole face lit up with joy. "The war is over" he repeated over and over again as if these were the only words that he knew.

How we cried as we sat there and ate sweet chocolate, not being able to take in what was happening, unable to believe that after so much suffering there could truly be an end in sight.

For the first time in over twelve months, I heard the beautiful song of birds and felt the cool breeze wash over me. Everyone was stunned at the thought the living hell we had endured the last year had finally come to an end and now we had to begin again.

Although a ceasefire had been called, it was to be a long time before we had free passage out of the town. Only aid convoys were allowed in and out to bring the much-needed basics including the water we had so frequently risked our lives to collect.

Novi Travnik's infrastructure and its people had been systematically and cruelly dragged into the ground. It was obvious to all who had survived the horror that it would take generations to rebuild the fabric and trust that had not only been sustained there, but had once flourished.

As this book draws to a close, so too do my own recollections, memories and feelings.

Regret is a strong emotion and one which is difficult to evade. My own personal regret in life is that Mom stayed behind in Bosnia when I myself left for America.

This regret will remain with me for the rest of my life, despite knowing she was happy that I was leaving for a new and we hoped, better life.

Thankfully, before her death she was able to meet my two young sons, Tony and Nino and got to enjoy their childish play and merriment.

My final words are that of a deep and heartfelt thank you to Mom for being there for me and giving me so much love in our lives together.

The memory of that will never fade with the passing of time and it pleases me now knowing connections have been made in life as in death.

"Thank you Mom. Your Nena."

\* \* \* \*

Vesna and brother Mile bravely facing the stark reality of the bloody war which had engulfed their country.

Fond farewells. Vesna pictured with her Mom Petra taken just before Vesna became Displaced to the United States of America.

Petra with husband Ilija taking respite with a game of chess. Vesna's father, before the war had been a keen player, winning many competitions.

Ostoja in his later years. The striking similarity in appearance to his lost brother Maksim increased with old age.

Happiness amidst the fear. Despite being under constant attack Vesna and Tonci married, even managing a smile for the camera.

Despite being sparsely populated, the funeral of Ostoja was attended my many. Mile proudly heads the cortège of his late Grandfather.

Lost brothers forever divided. The younger Maksim now lies at rest one thousand and fifty miles apart from the elder brother Ostoja

## Chapter Twenty Six - Time to heal

**Maybe it doesn't always rain** in Featherstone on Sunday. Maybe our minds select that particular memory to focus on, like the finest and darkest moments of our existence. Our minds are selective and pick out what really needs to be preserved for us to reminisce about in our later years. We only save what we want to for posterity and move the discarded fragments to one side, just out of sight and often forgotten; sometimes the truth is lost forever.

I saved the happy times; it was our "finest hour" that was preserved and remembered. In Vesna's case it was the happy times as well, but they remained tainted at the edges with the horrors of what she was exposed to.

My story is that of a childhood happiness I will never feel again. It is of idyllic days spent in the summer's sun, playing in the newly cut hay; natures very own playground. Those days have long since gone.

Even the song of the skylark is diminishing along with the memories of the past. Featherstone now would be an unrecognisable sight to Granddad. Long gone is the coalmine that gave birth to the town. The pastures of ripening hay now find themselves in constant retreat from the onslaught of concrete and newly erected houses.

The allotment has now all but disappeared. Once the pride of one man, the envy of many, it now adjoins a barren landscape making up a sanctuary for neglected horses.

The summerhouse, a place created for Nana to sit and enjoy, is no more. She would sit enjoying the summer sun, idly watching the man she loved as he worked the land.

There are many questions remaining to be answered surrounding her and one day I will finally piece together the full story. I will continue to scratch away at the surface and hope to fit the final pieces into the puzzle that was my grandparents.

Despite the small gaps and missing titbits, both Vesna and my own stories are connected through the love of two brothers, our grandfathers, at last reunited so long after their deaths. With the connection now made, we are hopeful the healing process can begin.

That said, in my experience, time does not always heal, but merely gives us the scope to recall and regret. My own regrets are many and, as the years pass, continually grow.

Probably the biggest regret I carry with me is I did not take Granddad up on his unexpected offer to record his life story.

The book was to be titled simply "Displaced People" and he was sure that it would be of interest to many people across the world.

I even remember him purchasing recording equipment in readiness. But my thoughts were focused on my own struggle, heavily caught up as I was in the yearlong miner's strike. I was young, full of energy and revelled in the prospect I would be a part of the revolt that was destined to be recorded in British history. Granddad's life story unfortunately, was to be left on hold.

I suspect Granddad had in fact carried on regardless with his project, as I would see the same recorder around the house from time to time.

After his death, a removal man tasked with clearing his possessions informed me a piece of furniture he was about to remove from the house had a drawer which was screwed shut. Neither thinking nor caring, I dismissed this and simply asked him to take the furniture regardless.

It was only weeks later, when the recording equipment could not be accounted for, that the realisation sank in. It was highly likely that if he had recorded his memories on tape, he would have hidden them as well as he had his thoughts.

There remain many questions which have been left unanswered and I fear now these have been irretrievably lost to the grave. Only when history is recorded can it then be passed down to the younger generations. If left, it disappears without a trace.

This book began in innocence and unknowing, the story of a child who held tight to the love of an elder he saw as invincible. As the child grew, so too did the invincibility of the man. When the reality of his demise truly hit home, the child had no choice but to take up this quest of hope, despair and finally triumph told in these pages.

Painstakingly slowly, the pieces of the puzzle were collected and fitted together to produce a picture which shows the lost world of the man he knew as Granddad Maksim.

At times it has been a painful process for both Vesna and myself to complete and record this text. Firstly, the pain and grief continues for the men we loved and secondly the horrors that Bosnia and her people suffered in those cruel years of the civil war haunt us, especially Vesna who of course suffered first hand.

We can but hope that enough of what was almost lost is preserved here for future generations to understand, remember and ultimately continue the story.

Granddad had retained the essence of his homeland and the memory of it pushed me on, every step of the way. Now the story is almost over, I feel as if the peace I recognise as Maksim is settling all around me. I have seen what he saw, from the rolling hillside scenery to the wooden houses and I have felt the love of the people there, just as he did. So many years since his death, I see him clearly now, his whole self, through the ever-loving eyes of a man now, instead of a child.

Vesna ultimately added her voice to the book for the love of her mom, Petra, the one who compelled her to put pen to paper, the one who had lived through the horrors of war, not once, but twice before her death in 2007. This book serves as a tribute to her, a way for Vesna to protect her memory the way her mother protected her during those harsh wartime years.

It is nice to imagine that the two brothers are somewhere together now, finally filling in their own blanks and reliving their childhood, talking, laughing and crying over what was and what could have been.

Perhaps their mother once again sits and watches them, playing in the rapids of the River Pliva, transported back to a far simpler time of games and hi-jinks, a time before war scarred Yugoslavia and then broke her apart.

Are they smiling as they sit once again on the grassy slopes of Brđani, sipping plum brandy and smoking crude cigarettes made from cornhusks? Do they know our family is finally complete again?

Whatever the truth, this book is an accurate account of a family torn apart through war and eventually bought back together through the determination of the younger generations, rallied on by love and a need to know the truth.

This is our family's story, recollections, and memories, finally written down, just as Maksim always wanted.

\* \* \* \*

Also by the same Authors

## When Spirits Break Free
Andy Evans & Vesna Kovac

Reality joins the unexplained in this gripping novel. From coal mining backgrounds to the horrors of drug induced psychosis to the realities of what could be.

Billy Hall was as humble as the very beginnings from those he was born into. Coal had been king and ruled the landscape surrounding the small town of Castlefields for countless generations.

From an early age, it was obvious to Molly her son did not fit into the mould expected for the traditions of children following their forefathers, deep down into the depths to win out the coals for a grateful nation.

Although Billy had been surrounded by children of his own age, parading, and playing out their games of fantasy along the cobbled streets, he more often chose his own company away from the others.

The friends of imagination that crept silently from the darkened shadows, provided him the friendship, and consolation, which sought more and more, as early childhood progressed.

Adolescence beckoned, and the shadows withdrew, leaving Billy to seek out his own amusement and friendship that the town offered.

Innocently, the key would be turned again, releasing those who had been lost, to once again emerge and make their presence felt.

With the door within his mind once again opened, Billy would be left to face his own ultimate destiny.

*'A beautiful piece of work. The gritty backdrop of the Yorkshire mining town provides a great setting for this most skilled of writers to weave his magic. As a Yorkshire man myself, the history of coal mining is fascinating. But then you become drawn in to a thriller that is not what you expect at all. The unexpected in this case is thrilling! Billy's journey is both haunting and magical. When the spirits Break Free is highly recommended!'*

Simon Swift - Author of Black Shadows

Available from Amazon and other online retailers.

Paperback, Hardcover and Kindle versions online.

www.ingramcontent.com/pod-product-compliance
Lightning Source LLC
Chambersburg PA
CBHW060111170426
43198CB00010B/845